GETTING YOUR HOUSE (AND LIFE) IN ORDER

GETTING YOUR HOUSE (AND LIFE) IN ORDER

Kate Redd, Connie Neal
& Steve Woodworth

Galahad Books   New York

Published in 1994 by

Galahad Books
A division of Budget Book Service, Inc.
386 Park Avenue South
New York, NY 10016

Galahad Books is a registered trademark of Budget Book Service, Inc.

Published by arrangement with Thomas Nelson Inc., Publishers.

Library of Congress Catalog Card Number: 93-80397

ISBN: 0-88365-859-3

Printed in the United States of America

Contents

I. Choose to Take Control

Dedicated to

My mother,
Catherine,

who taught me that order and spontaneity
are not opposites, but that one makes
possible the other, and that both
are to be desired and pursued

✔ Contents

Introduction:
It Doesn't Need
to Stay This
Way!

Are you feeling overwhelmed by too many obligations, too many loose ends, too many "things" to care for, too many bills?

Do you feel as if you have an "overstuffed life," with too much of just about everything, including too many things on your schedule and too many draws against your income?

This book is for you!

The good news for you today is that you *do* have control—probably more than you realize—over these three key areas of your life:

- your schedule,

- your money, and

- your possessions.

You *can* decide how you want to spend your time—at least the majority of it! Even if you work eight hours a day, you have the freedom to decide how you will spend your breaks and the hours each day when you aren't at work. You *can* decide how you want to spend your money. You *can* decide how much stuff you want to own, dust, collect, or store—and how much access you want to it.

To bring a sense of order to your life, you must first make these four decisions:

Choose to Take Control over your time, money, and possessions, rather than let these things control you. The fact is, if you don't take control, you will be controlled.

Choose to Strike a New Balance between input and output, income and expense, incoming and outgoing. We're all involved in a balancing act. We have twenty-four hours a day given to us; we choose how to divide that time into smaller segments and to spend it on various activities. We each have an income; we choose what and how much to purchase with it. We create a "space" for ourselves and decide how to fill it. The more we try to put into a space, get from an income, or do in a day, the more difficult it is to keep a sense of order and balance.

Choose to Put Like Things Together

Keeping like things together is perhaps the greatest thing you can do to achieve a sense of order in your life. As you begin to tackle the challenge of adding more order to your house and life, keep the word *clusters* in mind. Group things together. Store like things together. Put similar tasks together. Cluster errands and chores.

Choose Joy!   If you don't experience a sense of joy and fulfillment from a task, activity, relationship, purchase, process, or possession, let go of it. The purpose for bringing order to your life is not so that you can take on more, acquire more, or do more, but so that you can experience more joy.

Finally, it's important to recognize that every person has a different level of need for order. You may be able to handle a fuller schedule, more details, and more clutter than others. If you are sharing space, schedules, and money with someone, you'll need to find a compromise point. Recognize at the outset that there's no ideal "limit" to the number of pieces, time segments, or units that a person can accommodate successfully. Some people need very few things to feel an inner sense of balance and joy; others need more. Accommodate these differences as best you can. Don't be obsessive in your need for order. At the same time, do gain the sense of order that *you* need to feel control, balance, access, and joy.

Always remember, the number one reason for bringing order to something is so that you can use it and enjoy it to the fullest.

THE BIGGIES

Nine suggestions for gaining
order in the "big picture" of your life

1 ✔ Make a Budget

The best way to gain control over your money and possessions is to make a budget.

Most people know the basics of budget-making, but a surprising number of people have never been taught how to make a budget that reflects a personal financial plan. Let's review the basics.

Decide the Time Frame for Your Budget Most people deal with money on a monthly basis. Others find that a quarterly budget suits them best. For others, an annual or semi-annual overview gives order. If you are planning a two-week vacation, you may want to make a budget to cover only that time period.

If you are self-employed, or have income that fluctuates from month to month, you may find that it helps to make both monthly and quarterly budgets.

List All Your Sources of Income Make two categories: the "sure" sources, and the "possible" sources. If there's at least a twenty-percent chance that the amount won't be there in a given time frame, put it in the "possible" category. In constructing your budget, consider that you will only receive eighty percent of your income in the "possible" category. If you find at the end of the month that you've got more income than anticipated, set aside a portion of it for additional taxes and then use the remainder for investments.

If you are self-employed, you need to make certain that a portion of every income check is set aside for quarterly tax payments.

List Your Expenses   Begin with your fixed expenses. These are amounts that remain the same from month to month. Then, estimate those items that tend to fluctuate, such as utilities, food, gasoline, phone, clothing, and so forth. Don't overlook these key areas among your expenses:

•   *Contributions.* Many people pledge to give a set amount to their church or other not-for-profit organization on a regular basis. Include that figure among your fixed expenses.

•   *Savings.* Include savings in the fixed category, even if it's a small amount. Pay yourself this amount off the top and put it into a separate, interest-bearing account.

•   *Annualized or Periodic Payments.* This is an area that many people fail to budget properly. As a result, they find themselves in a cash-flow crunch.

In order to get a handle on this area of your finances, make a list of all of your anticipated annual or semiannual expenses, such as insurance premiums, car maintenance, etc.

If you are saving for a major purchase, such as an appliance, piece of furniture, or vehicle, add that item to your list. If you are saving for a child's college education, also add the amount you want to save to this list.

Add all of these amounts together, as best you can estimate them, and then divide by twelve. This gives you the amount each month that you need to set aside. Put this money into an interest-bearing checking or savings account. Then, when these expenses roll around, pay them from this separate account.

Credit Cards   Avoid their use. Your life will become a lot simpler, and probably less expensive. If you use credit cards, aim to pay them off.

2 ✔ Make a Will

One of the most difficult things for many people to do, and yet one of the most important for getting your life in order, is to make a will. Don't think of your will as something morbid or sad. Think of it strictly in financial-planning, possession-planning, and people-caring terms.

By planning for your departure from this world, you'll be helping those you love in a tremendous way, releasing them from the burden of making major decisions in their sorrow, saving them unnecessary expense, and making sure that each person you want to remember materially is properly regarded. Furthermore, by making decisions about your death when you are healthy, you are saving yourself the added emotional burden that can arise in having to face such decisions while battling a serious illness or injury.

Your Legal Will Work with an attorney in constructing your will. Although many self-help forms are available and can give you a good start in making your plans, you should still consult an attorney. An attorney will be able to ask you questions about issues you may not have considered, and also be able to suggest alternatives and innovative methods of planning your estate.

A Living Will Decide whether you want to have a living will. This document states that if the situation should arise in which there is no reasonable expectation of your recovery from physical or mental disability, you request that you be allowed to die and not be kept alive by artificial means or heroic measures. Most physicians and clergymen have forms, as do attorneys.

Disposition of Your Body Do you want to donate your body organs for transplant purposes to help others? Do you want to give your body to help medical schools in their research and in training of future physicians? Do you wish to be buried, or cremated?

Funeral Arrangements It will take you less than an hour to plan your funeral, and save your loved ones a great deal of anguish. List your favorite Scriptures or readings, your choice of flowers and music. State whom you would like to conduct the service or have part in it (including pallbearers, soloists, organist). Describe the nature of the service (memorial service, graveside service, closed-casket).

General Information In a file along with your will, living will, and funeral arrangements, you may want to provide this information for your survivors:

- Obituary information. Jot down key dates, places, and events of your life, as well as the names of all close relatives.

- Location of key documents, bank accounts, insurance policies, name of attorney.

- A list of persons to notify about your death.

- A list of any bequests you'd like to see made beyond the scope of your will. You may have small personal items of sentimental value that you'd like to go to specific persons. Bear in mind that, unless these items are stated in your formal will, the bequests you desire are not legally binding.

You may want to discuss this information with others in your family. Or, you may simply want to let key members of your family know that you have made such plans. Let them know where they can find the file of your final wishes after your death.

Once you have a will and a set of final wishes in place, you'll probably experience a great sense of relief and a feeling that something important has been put in order.

3 ✔ Keep Important Documents in a Safe Place

Every person needs a safe place to keep important documents. You may want to have a locked, fire-proof safe installed in your basement or an interior closet. Have your key documents grouped together in this safe for quick access.

A safety deposit box in a local bank or savings organization is perhaps the best place to keep your important documents, or at least a copy of them. You may also want to have a copy of key documents on file in the home of a close relative.

Ask yourself, "If I had only ten minutes to evacuate my home, could I put my hands on key documents within the first sixty seconds?" Ask:

- What do I need to have, should my house be completely destroyed?

- What do I need to be able to put my hands on, should I not have access to my house?

Hotel Safety Deposit Boxes   When traveling, take advantage of the safety deposit boxes provided by hotels for your key belongings (such as passport, traveler's checks, and jewelry).

4 ✔ Reappraise Your Insurance Coverage

Periodically reappraise your insurance coverage. The need for various types of insurance fluctuates greatly during a lifetime. Types of insurance policies being offered tend to vary greatly from decade to decade.

Don't assume that your insurance agent automatically will want to talk you into increasing your coverage if you make an appointment to discuss your policies. If that's your first assumption, consider finding a new agent! You may want to seek out a general financial planner who includes insurance as only one aspect of a broader financial planning service.

Focus on the details of your current situation and your current policies. Think in terms of your needs during the next three-to-five years, then reevaluate. Ask:

Do I Need This Insurance? Weigh the risks of not having a particular type of insurance. For example, if you have no dependents and no large debts or mortgages for which you are responsible, you should seriously weigh your need for life insurance. If you are self-employed, consider your need for long-term disability insurance.

Which Type of Financial Vehicle Is Best? Insurance is not the only vehicle that provides income to beneficiaries, or a source of money against which to borrow in emergencies. Weigh the pros and cons of whole-life policies versus term insurance. Have someone list the advantages and disadvantages for you in clear, easily understood terms. Don't think in terms of national averages or typical cases; evaluate the coverage and benefits in terms of your own life and needs. Nobody knows your total financial picture better than you do. Ask a financial planner about alternatives to insurance in providing for retirement income. Ask about other ways of planning your estate to benefit your survivors.

Are My Deductibles Too Low? If you are paying premiums for the lowest possible deductible on the highest amount of coverage, the chances are that you will pay out a great deal more than you will ever recover in claims. In fact, if you make too many low-deductible claims, you may find your policy being cancelled or your rates increased. Use insurance not as a means of covering small accidents or losses, but of covering major illnesses, injuries, or losses. Your savings account should be built up enough to cover small losses.

Is My Coverage Adequate? If you have young children, and both you and your spouse are working to make ends meet, you probably will need more life insurance than if you and your spouse are both retired or your children are through their formal schooling and are financially independent. If you are retirement age, weigh the possibilities of supplemental health insurance policies that extend coverage beyond what Medicare will pay.

Social Security Request a statement from the Social Security Administration every three-to-five years. Forms are available at your local Social Security office. The statement will tell you how much has been credited to your account. Compare that figure to the totals that have been deducted from your payroll checks, or your self-employment deposits. Keep in mind that human error is always possible in recording information; computers are only as good as those who input the raw data.

Insurance Files Keep all your insurance policies together in your filing system for quick access. Duplicate copies of summary pages for policies and keep them in your safety deposit box or fireproof files. Include as part of your files proof that the current premiums have been paid.

5 ✔ Plan for Your Retirement

Most people dream of their retirement years in terms of how they'd like to spend their time and where they'd like to live or travel. The keys to a successful retirement are having the health to enjoy one's retirement years and the money to pay for what one chooses to do. Both health and finances take planning, not dreaming.

The time to plan for your retirement is now, no matter how young you may be.

Set Specific Retirement Goals Set a specific annual income. List a particular locale where you'd like to retire. As a part of your plan, state how you'd like to live—the amount of energy and health you want to have, and what activities you specifically want to be able to do.

You need to have a target to aim at! Only with specific goals can you map out a specific plan for reaching them.

Balance Your Current Need for Cash and Your Future Need for Security You obviously need to live between now and the day you retire. Develop a strategy that balances your current needs and your eventual goals. If you are young, you will probably want to consider the purchase of a home as a long-range investment that can help secure your retirement later.

Develop a Retirement Fund   Be certain it accrues tax-free.

A Strategy for Long-Term Wellness   Retirement means very little unless you have good health to enjoy those years. Health takes planning. Make an appointment with your family physician solely to discuss preventive health care strategies.

Your personal family physician can help you map out a strategy of exercise, diet, and personal habits that has the best possible likelihood of not only extending the length of your life, but the quality of your life.

Planning for your future helps to order your current financial and fiscal fitness regimen. In setting goals and planning strategies for retirement, you will come to grips with your current financial and physical needs, goals, and habits. Thinking in terms of retirement is like drawing the outline to a picture. It gives you a framework for making individual choices about how to color in or define the details of your present life. Without such an outline, it's difficult to make long-range choices or to build life-long habits.

6 ✔ Conduct a Household Inventory

As a precursor to planning for your home insurance needs, you will want to develop a thorough household inventory.

House Plan Keep a copy of your house plans, or make a scale drawing. Not only will this be valuable to you in event of damage to your home, but you will find it helpful should you need to make repairs or wish to remodel.

Photographic Coverage One of the easiest ways to do a household inventory is with a still or video camera. Photograph every area of your house so that all appliances and pieces of furniture are visible. Also photograph the exterior of your home, including any patio or poolside furniture, and any buildings or storage areas that are not attached to your house. Label each photo by room and correlate it to a written description.

You may want to give this job to a budding young camera buff in your family.

A Written Description   Provide a written description of each major item in your home. If possible, provide the cost of the item when purchased, and the year of purchase. If you have inherited or purchased antiques, give as much information about an item as you can. If an item has a serial number, record it.

Jewelry and Personal Items   Photograph and describe all pieces of jewelry or valuable personal clothing.

Collections   If you have a collection, describe it thoroughly, and photograph it.

Don't overlook your family library as a collection. List the titles to all of your books, records, videotapes, cassettes, and compact discs. Use $3'' \times 5''$ cards, so that you can put your inventories into alphabetical order or specific categories. Estimate the total number of books or other items you own and give an average dollar figure to each item. (The cost of replacing a library or music collection is going to be much more than you have probably anticipated!)

Vehicles   Be sure to include descriptions of your vehicles, including outdoor equipment such as lawn mowers.

Other Property If you own vacation property or rental properties, make a periodic inventory of them. A set of interior photographs prior to the renting of property to others can provide solid evidence should a dispute arise about the refunding of a cleaning or security deposit.

Receipts Keep receipts for major items of furniture or valuable antiques, paintings, and jewelry.

Updates You'll want to update your household inventory at least once every three-to-five years, or as you make additional major purchases. Keep a copy of the photos or videotape, and the accompanying written description, in your safety deposit box.

7 ✔ Put It on the Calendar

Gaining a sense of control over time and getting your schedule in order require one basic tool: a calendar. Buy or make a calendar that meets your needs. You may need a calendar that breaks a day down into fifteen-minute increments; you may need a calendar that allows only a little bit of space for each day. You'll want a calendar that allows you to plan your activities most effectively. For example, you may want a calendar that shows an entire week at a time, or a month, or a quarter, or a year.

Focus on one calendar format for recording your commitments. For example, if your calendar shows a week at a time, you may still want to have annual or quarterly calendars available for reference. Record all your commitments only on the weekly format calendar. Don't attempt to juggle more than one calendar format at a time. Even more important, limit yourself to one personal calendar. Don't have a calendar at home and another at work. Keep one calendar and carry it with you or have ready access to it at home, at work, and as you travel.

Family Calendars   You may find it necessary to have a master family calendar in addition
to your personal calendar. If so, develop a habit of
going over that calendar on a regular basis—
weekly or daily—with other members of the family, to make certain that everyone knows when
and where they need to be. Have a periodic Family Calendar Pow-Wow, in which every member of
the family goes over the upcoming week's events,
or looks ahead to an entire month or season. This
can be especially beneficial as you enter a holiday
season, or anticipate the events of summer.

A Commitment to Scheduling   Discuss
those events that may be happening in your community, church, or other groups to which you belong, and make a decision about whether you
want to participate. If you'd like to keep the event
as an option, you may want to write it down in
parentheses or label it as a *maybe*.

Calendar Control   You control the calendar;
the calendar doesn't control you. If you find that
you or your family is feeling over-scheduled or
over-committed, get out the eraser and free up
some time.

8 ✔ Write It Down!

Perhaps the single most beneficial thing you can do to add order to your life is to develop a habit of writing lists. Not only will you be freeing up memory space in your own brain, you'll gain a better handle on how to structure your time, finances, and possessions.

A List Is a Tool The reason for a list is to help you remember to do something, or to help you make a decision. There's nothing that's too big or small for a list, if such a list is *helpful* to you.

Cluster and Prioritize One of the most helpful aspects of list-making is that it allows you to cluster like activities together, and then to prioritize them.

- List all of your calls. At the same time, decide whom you need to call first.

- List all the things you need to do this morning. As you list them, decide what order to do them in.

- List the projects you need to complete. You now have the basic foundation needed for dividing tasks into doable steps, setting periodic deadlines, and juggling more than one project at once.

Side-by-side lists of personal things to do and professional things to do can help you balance your home and work lives. Listing the things you hope to complete in a week can help you pare down and prioritize your work load.

A list can also help you develop a new habit. If there's something you'd like to make a part of your daily routine, list it! You'll be focusing your attention on that task and there's a far greater likelihood that you'll make time for it. A time of morning prayer, kissing your spouse before you leave for work, telling your child you love her, flossing at night—no habit is too small to list if it's truly something you consider important to your life.

Completing a List   Don't feel compelled to complete a list before you revise it, make a new one, or add to it. Lists aren't records of accomplishment; they are tools for planning, prioritizing, and scheduling. Don't become so list absorbed that you spend all of your creative energy writing down what you want to do, and then fail to get in gear and do those things. A list is only as good as the results it produces.

9 ✔ Live Free of Guilt and Bitterness

All of the planning, sorting, and organizing you do won't help you live an ordered life if you don't find a way of dealing with guilt and bitterness. Guilt stems from what you feel *you* should have done, or shouldn't have done. Bitterness grows from a feeling that *someone else* should or shouldn't have done something.

The real purpose for having order in life is to develop a sense of control over the controllables, and a resulting feeling of balance, accomplishment, and joy. Nothing robs a person of control, balance, fulfillment, or joy, as much as guilt and bitterness.

Eliminating Guilt and Bitterness The only way to get rid of guilt and bitterness is through forgiveness. Forgiveness begins with recognition that you have said or done something that violates your concept of the type of person you really want to be. Face up to that shortfall. If it's a sin against your Creator, apologize and ask for help in not repeating the offense. If it's a sin against your neighbor, apologize and seek to make amends.

Once you have a sense of forgiveness from God, forgive yourself and get on with your life. Don't live in the past or let the past cast a shadow on your future. If you ask forgiveness of a person who refuses to forgive you or refuses to allow you to make amends, face up to the fact that you have done all you can do. Move forward in your life.

Forgiveness Brings Order to a Relationship   It heals. It restores. There's an accompanying sense of freedom, which allows a person to face the future with a positive outlook. New choices can be made that can bring a greater sense of balance, fulfillment, and joy.

SPACE CONTROL

Seven suggestions for bringing
order to your space

10 ✔ Forming Clusters

A major key in ordering your possessions is to put like things together in a separate container or area.

Containers A variety of containers can be used for sorting items of all types. Use your imagination! Clear plastic sweater boxes, clean tool boxes, cash boxes, or artist supply boxes can all be used in innovative ways. Baby food jars are excellent containers for buttons, safety pins and straight pins, paper clips, picture-hanging nails, and other small items. Baskets are excellent for clustering pens and pencils, sewing or hobby supplies, magazines, photographs, stationery, hair ornaments, or business cards. Plastic file boxes, rolling baskets, and various types of bins can be used for storing children's art supplies, toys, and books, clothing, office supplies, and craft projects. Large mugs or short wide vases can be used for holding wooden spoons, cooking utensils, paint brushes, or makeup brushes. Blanket storage boxes can be used for storing winter sweaters and sporting gear.

Dividers   Cutlery dividers can be used to sort makeup and beauty supplies in bathroom drawers. Dividers in a clothing drawer can keep socks from undies. Also consider cupboard dividers that might create half shelves. In a kitchen cabinet, a half-shelf divider can be very useful in organizing spices for easy accessibility—or you might consider a drawer divider designed for just that use. A vertical divider in the cupboard over a refrigerator can be a useful device for sorting trays. In a bureau, armoire, or bedroom cupboard, stacking dividers can be used for separating various items of clothing or bed and bath linens.

Shelves   Think of shelves as being capable of holding and organizing far more than books. A shelf over your washer and dryer can be used for holding all of your laundry products. A kitchen shelf can hold a collection of teapots or cookbooks, freeing up cupboard and counter space. Shelving in a closet provides a useful means of organizing shoes, purses, and hats. A bathroom shelf can hold a stack of towels.

Wall Units   A Peg-board with hooks is an excellent device in a child's room for organizing coats, umbrellas, hats. In a kitchen, some types of racks can be used for suspending pots, pans, or for hanging mugs and cooking utensils.

Specialty Units   Various types of shoe trees or shoe bags can be placed on the backs of closet doors. A wide variety of items termed "organizers," valets, caddies, or racks are available.

Clustering Hints

- Use only one container per type of item. Have one container for all your spools of thread, not five.

- Use items you already have. Chances are, you already have enough boxes, bins, and baskets to put more than half of your unorganized possessions into order.

- When buying additional storage items, look for durability, adjustability, and stackability.

Remember: a place for everything and everything in its place. Get items grouped together. And keep those items grouped together. Teach your children at an early age that when they are finished using an item, they must put it back in its place. Develop that habit yourself.

11 ✔ Designating Spaces

The second step related to clustering is to designate spaces for certain activities. Every home tends to need these four designated spaces:

A Place for Arrival Every house or apartment has a main entrance for family use. Within that area, you need a place to dump what you bring in from the outside world, whether it's a briefcase, an arm load of grocery sacks, or a dripping umbrella. Consider the old-fashioned back porch. It had many features still needed today by virtually all families.

- A place to clean your shoes, or remove your shoes. A washable floor mat and a shoe rack can help keep the rest of your house cleaner.

- A place to hang a wet garment or stash a wet umbrella. Umbrella stands and plastic-coated peg racks are good ideas.

- A table for temporarily placing what is in your hands. This table can also be used for

items that need to be taken out, such as
school lunch pails.

- A bin for wet or soiled garments.

- A bin or basket for depositing trash
  brought in from outside, or your car.

- A paper towel rack for your ready use in
  dealing with spills or messes best left on
  the porch and not brought into the rest of
  the house.

Let your "arrival spot" become your first line of
defense for organizing and ordering your gear.

A Place to Eat For as many meals as possible, limit your family's dining to a specific place,
such as the kitchen counter or table. Not only will
cleaning up after meals be easier, but you'll avoid
messy spills in other areas of the house that take
time, and sometimes money, to clean.

A Place for Projects Have a designated
space for sewing, craft projects, and hobbies, preferably a room or area of a room with a large work
surface. Limit the number of projects that can be
ongoing at any one time, and also limit the
amount of time the work space can be occupied
by that project. If you don't place limitations on
the work space, you might find that you have a
doll house under construction in the corner of

the kitchen for six months, or that every room of the house has a craft project in progress.

A Place to Play   Every room in your house need not be considered a playroom. Limit your child to a specific room for play, and insist that each game or toy be put away promptly when the child is finished with it. You'll save yourself a lot of headaches and hassle if you help your children develop the habit of putting away one toy or game before moving on to a new one.

12 ✔ Designating Places

You'll save yourself hours of roaming your home or rummaging through pockets and purses if you have designated places for these three must-have-right-now items:

Keys Install a key rack in your kitchen or porch area, a place where you can keep all the keys of all family members. Get in the habit of putting your keys there as soon as you walk in the door.

Limit yourself to one set of keys that you take with you from home to work or on errands, and back. Include in that set all of the keys that you need on a daily or regular basis. Keep other keys, which are used only periodically, on separate rings. Label every set of keys.

Should you find that you are frequently locking yourself out of your home or car, keep a second set of keys on your car (such as in a magnetized holder that can be hidden in the engine area or under the frame) or at your home (perhaps under a specified rock or taped to the underside of a planter).

Eyeglasses or Contact Lenses Have a designated place for your reading glasses, sunglasses, and your spare pair of glasses or contact lenses. When you take off a pair of glasses, put them immediately in the place you have designated. Choose a place that protects your eyewear. If you travel a great deal, have a place for putting your extra eyeware (in a briefcase, suitcase, or the glove compartment of your car). Make sure you have sturdy eyewear holders.

Hearing Aids and Dentures When you remove your hearing aid or dentures, immediately put them in a designated space—one in which they will not only be safe, but remain clean.

Other Quick-Access Items Several other items also seem to call for a designated place of their own. *Pocket change:* a small coin purse can be a valuable item to tuck into the glove compartment of your car; refill it periodically with change from your wallet so that you will always have money for parking meters or tolls. *Car registration and proof of insurance:* have a designated place within your car for holding your car registration and proof of insurance. *Claim tickets:* have a special place for all of your claim checks; that way, when you get ready to go pick up the items you've taken in for service or processing, you'll be able to find the stubs you need quickly and easily.

13 ✔ Cleaning Out

As you begin to cluster items together, set up five containers labeled as follows:

- *Throw away.* You can use your normal trash bin for this one.

- *Give away.* A big, sturdy box or two will probably suffice. You may want to have one box for specific give-aways (to relatives or friends), and one box for charity donations.

- *Recycle.* You may need several sacks or boxes for this area—one each for glass, plastic, paper, and aluminum.

- *Repair.* Make certain that items you put into this pile are ones you want to keep, items that can be repaired, and items that are cost-effective to repair (as opposed to buying a new item). A word of caution about repair containers. They can remain filled for a long time, and become just another box or basket of clutter. Make a deal with yourself that if an item remains in a repair container for longer than three

months, you'll shift it over to the throw-
away container.

- *Return.* When you begin a serious effort at
  bringing order to your home or apartment,
  you'll probably be amazed at how many
  items you have that are borrowed and need
  to be returned. Label each item with a strip
  of masking tape, indicating to whom it belongs, and put yourself on a schedule for
  returning the things that aren't yours.

As each container becomes full, deal with it. If
it's trash, put it out for collection. If it's for charity,
seal up the box and deliver it. If it's recyclable,
bag it, put it into the trunk of your car, and drive
to the depository.

Four Key Questions to Ask   As you begin
to cluster a particular category or possession,
evaluate each item before it goes into its new container. Ask yourself these four questions:

- Have I used this in the past two years?

- Can I anticipate a specific time (function,
  event, or reason) to use this within the next
  two years?

- Does this item give me aesthetic pleasure?

- Does this item have value as an heirloom,
  or am I saving it for a specific person? (Be

> sure you can name the person to whom you
> expect to give the item.)

Unless you can answer yes to at least one of
these questions, discard the item and don't think
twice about it. Face up to the fact that you probably never will need it. And no, it probably won't be
worth a lot of money someday. No matter what
you paid for the item initially, if you aren't using
it, don't derive aesthetic pleasure from it, or don't
consider it to be of heirloom value, there's really
no reason for you to keep it. Give it to someone
who can use it or who will enjoy it.

Clutter-Elimination Motivators   The
best motivator for removing clutter is to work at
the task with others. Provide a means of rewarding yourself or family for getting rid of the
clutter. You might set up a scale and record the
number of pounds of stuff you give away, throw
away, or otherwise eliminate. Set up a reward system in advance according to the number of
pounds you eliminate—perhaps a family outing to
a movie, beach, or concert.

Keep your eyes focused clearly on the goal:
eliminating excess in order to have more access
to the things that you truly use, need, and enjoy
having around.

14 ✔ Clothing Control

We tend not to wear or use things we don't see, so the number-one principle in organizing a closet is this: have all items in full view.

Use shoe boxes that are clear, or remove the ends of cardboard boxes and stack them. Use shoe bags for holding stockings, scarves, gloves, or rolled-up belts. Add enough storage bins or shelving so that you can readily see your folded sweaters, hats, and purses.

Divide and Conquer Get organized by dividing your clothing in these four ways:

- Separate your nonclothing items from your clothing, and remove all nonclothing items from your closet or drawers.

- Separate your closet and drawer space into your space and any space you may share with a spouse, roommate, or sibling.

- Separate your in-season clothing from out-of-season clothing. Put the in-season clothing at the front of your closet or drawer space. As the seasons change, move appropriate garments into the up-front position.

- Separate clothing by type: formal and casual. Hang coordinating elements within close proximity. You may find that you are visually able to put together looks that you didn't realize you were capable of creating.

Twice a year, or at the change of seasons, reevaluate your clothing. If an item is worn or faded beyond repair or use, discard it. If you haven't worn the item in the past two years or if the item has outlived its style, give it away.

Realize that garments need space in order to breathe. Your clothes will last longer, smell better, and require less cleaning and ironing if you give each garment enough room to hang freely.

Repair-and-Clean Basket When you find an item of clothing that needs repair or cleaning, separate it immediately from your other garments and put it in a designated laundry basket. Then take those items to the cleaners or shoe repair shop as soon as possible. If an item needs hemming or mending, deal with it as quickly as you can schedule a repair hour. You'll save yourself a great deal of frustration if you keep the garments in your wardrobe ready to wear.

15 ✔ Pantry and Cupboard Control

You can apply to your kitchen many of the same techniques you have used to bring order to your wardrobe.

Kitchen cupboards have a way of harboring little-used or outdated items, from small appliances to old spices. Ask yourself about appliances:

- Have I used this item in the last year?

- Can I think of a specific time I will use it during the coming six months?

If your answer is no to both questions, that item should go out the door. Also ask yourself, "How many of this item do I have?" You may be surprised to find that you have more than one potato masher or cheese grater, or that you have three jars of cumin powder among your spices. If you have excess, get rid of it.

In bringing order to kitchen cupboards, the rule of thumb is this: if you can't reach it, you won't use it. Bring into easy reach all the items that you need or use on a regular basis. You should be able to reach within one or two steps all you need to prepare an average meal.

Hard-to-Reach Areas   Reserve the top shelves of your cupboards for dishes and glassware you only use on special occasions. You can also stash your unused extras on the top shelves; for example, if you have twelve plates but use four of them, keep four on a lower shelf, and put the other eight on the top shelf. Consider a half-shelf divider and use the extra space for the bowls or glasses you use most often.

Storage for Perishables   Make certain you have sufficient storage containers for items that need to be kept airtight or sealed. Choose see-through containers that are stackable. Cannister lids should fit tightly.

Five Basic Tips   Here are five tips for saving time and effort, and for bringing order to kitchen disorder:

- *Keep your work surface as clear as possible.* If you have to remove items from a counter-top or table before you can use it, find another place for those items.

- *Clean up as you go.* Don't let the dishes pile high. Rinse them and put them into the dishwasher before the food has time to stick.

- *Use a dishwasher-safe spoon rest or small tray for tea bags and cooking spoons and utensils.*

- *Cluster items.* Keep your canned goods together. Cluster the items you need for baking, and cluster the utensils you use when baking. Stack items that come in floppy pouches, such as beans, soup mixes, and dried foods, or toss them into a stackable bin in a pantry area.

- *Think in terms of cubic space in your cupboards and under your cupboards.* Use shelf dividers and stacking units. Hang cups and mugs from the underside of cupboard shelves. If counter space is a premium, consider appliances that attach to the bottom of cabinets.

Safety First   Make certain that kitchen cleansers, bug sprays, and other poisonous items are kept out of reach of young children. Toddler-proof your lower cupboards and drawers with safety latches. Keep the trash can away from curious toddlers. Consider installing burn-guards for your stove top. Make certain that you have a fire extinguisher within easy access to your stove—but out of the reach of young children—and that you know how to use it.

16 ✔ A Place for Tools and Equipment

The three tools most frequently used by most people are few in number and very simple to store: a hammer, a screwdriver, and a pair of pliers. If these and a few other simple devices (tape measure, level, and wire cutters) are all you have, you can easily store these items in a shoe box that's clearly labeled. Unfortunately, most of us have a tool collection that goes far beyond these basics!

You may want to designate a drawer for the small items that we all seem to need periodically, such as batteries, picture hangers, and spare fuses. Most other tools can be stored in a garage or area over a workbench using a Peg-board and hooks.

If you need space for tools and don't have a garage or extra closet space, you may want to consider buying a footlocker or trunk (one you can lock). Such an item can be used as a coffee table, be covered with a fabric skirt and become a "specialty" table, or simply be stashed in the corner of a room as a decorative item. Guests need never guess the contents!

Yard and Garden Equipment In storing yard and garden equipment, make certain the equipment is not accessible to young children. Gasoline and other types of fuels, as well as insecticides, gardening supplies, fertilizers, and de-icing agents should be stored properly. Cluster these items together on shelves. A locked cabinet can be a useful unit for storing small equipment and garden supplies in a garage.

Bicycles Use racks in your garage to store bicycles. A bicycle that is hung, suspended, or kept vertical takes up less space than one that is laid on its side. Cluster items required for bike repair and equipment used for biking safety.

MONEY CONTROL

Four specific ways to put more
order into your finances

17 ✔ Shop Specifically

"Just browsing" generally translates into wasted money, unfocused time, and unwanted possessions. Impulse buying does more to torpedo a carefully plotted financial plan than any other single action over which you can exert control. Here are four strategies for helping you avoid the gotta-have-it-right-now syndrome:

Shop with Lists Make a written list before you shop, and discipline yourself to stick to the list. This principle applies to all purchases, not just groceries. Keep tucked into your purse three ongoing lists:

- *The year-round-gift-shopping list.* On this list, have the names of people you anticipate "gifting" during the holiday season, or for birthdays, anniversaries, or other special occasions. (Ideally, next to each name you have put a dollar figure based on the annualized budget you prepared in chapter 1.) Should you see an item that you think is a perfect gift for a person for a specific occasion, check your list to make certain that you haven't already purchased something for that person, check the price against your proposed budget for both the gift and the amount you intended to spend that month on gifts, and if all signals are green, go for it.

- *The wardrobe-needs list.* As you have organized your clothing in chapter 14, and have reevaluated your wardrobe needs each season, you have discovered some gaps in your wardrobe that you'd like to fill. Those needs can be subjected to the same process as purchasing a gift. Does it fit your need, your budget?

- *The waiting-for-it-to-go-on-sale list.* Think through the things you find yourself purchasing year after year—from holiday greeting cards to garden fertilizer. Make a list of them. Then attempt to purchase these items when they go on sale.

Avoid the Unexpected "Discount" Temptation
Many times we see items on sale and find the savings irresistible. Rather than look at the savings, look at the remaining dollar figure. Is the item something you really need? Is the money for this item in your budget? No matter how good the bargain, if you don't need the item right away or can't afford it, it's not a good purchase. The same goes for coupons. Even if the

manufacturer offers you a dollar off, if the item isn't one you use or need, why spend $4 to save $1?

Shop with a Dollar Limit and Take Cash
You can avoid the tendency to splurge or purchase on impulse by consulting your budget before you go shopping, and setting a dollar limit on the amount you will spend for that particular outing. Then take just that much cash with you and leave all your credit cards at home. You'll find it more difficult to part with cash or to write a check than to spend "plastic money," and those extra few moments of hesitation may give you just the time you need to rethink an impulsive decision.

Avoid Shopping in "Clutter Traps"
Avoid those places that cry out to you to purchase items that you are going to call *clutter* six months from now. These include souvenir shops or garage sales and flea markets. If you are collecting a specific type of object or are seeking to complete an antique set of china or silver, be sure you take a specific list with you and refuse to be tempted by anything else.

18 ✔ Research Your Major Purchases

Major purchases can range from an appliance to a piece of furniture to a vehicle to a new fall suit. The definition of *major* is up to you. A new coffeemaker or a new toaster may be a purchase well worth a little research.

Begin Your Research at Home Start your purchasing research at home. Before going out to shop for back-to-school clothes, take a look at what still fits each child, what might be passed down from one child to the next, and what can be updated with new accessories. Make a list of what you *have,* rather than what you *need.*

In preparing for the purchase of an appliance or piece of furniture measure the space where you anticipate placing the item. (No need to shop for a baby grand piano if you only have room for an upright!) Ask what best suits your needs.

Consult the Experts Look through magazines to get ideas about ways in which you might fit a new purchase into your existing environment. Keep in mind that the rooms pictured in magazines are likely to be bigger than those in your home or apartment.

Consider the performance level of an item. Has the item been evaluated by a magazine that compares and rates products? Take time to visit your public library and read these reviews.

Consider your friends and associates to be user-friendly and user-wise experts. Ask what they have purchased and how satisfied they are.

Ask Questions of the Salesman How does this model compare to other models or brands? Have you had any of these items returned? Why? What warranty is included? Where can the item be serviced? Think in terms of performance first; from among those near-equals, choose the style you like.

Try It Out Just as you'd try on a coat before buying it, try out an appliance or take a vehicle for a test drive before you make a decision. Don't let the salesman push the vacuum cleaner on the showroom floor carpet; *you* push it. Does it feel right to *you*? Can you maneuver it easily? Can you attach the accessories easily? Lie down on the mattress. Sit on the sofa.

Comparison Shop Don't fall victim to the first salesman you encounter. Even after carefully conducting your home and expert research, make a commitment to evaluating—on site—at least three different brands or models, preferably in three different stores.

19 ✔ Buy Quality

A better quality item will probably last longer and provide more satisfaction than an item of less quality. Style and brand name may or may not be equated with quality; a high price tag doesn't ensure it. Quality is generally based on these factors:

- *Material used in construction.* Are you dealing with hardwood or fiberboard? What type of stuffing has been used? What is the spring construction? How much steel has been used? Is the fabric tightly or loosely woven?

- *Sturdiness of construction.* Are the joints of a piece of furniture notched together or glued? Are the seams tightly stitched?

- *Durability or life expectancy.* How long does the manufacturer expect the item to last? In the experience of your friends, experts, and even the salesman, how long does the item actually last?

- *Smoothness of operation.* Do the working parts fit together well and run smoothly?

Ask about the number of working parts; the fewer the parts, the less chance of breakage.

- *Manufacturer's reliability.* Find out who manufactures the item you are seeking to buy. What is their reputation for quality in the industry?

New or Used   Quality isn't necessarily dependent on the age of an item. A better gauge is the amount of use against the total life expectancy of the item. A luxury car that is two years old and has been well maintained may be a much wiser, more cost-effective purchase than a new economy car.

The Wise-Purchase Rule   A simple purchasing rule to keep in mind is this: *Purchase the greatest amount of quality that you can within your budget.* In purchasing quality, you are likely to find yourself reducing quantity. Fewer items of better quality tend to equal less clutter, wiser use of money, savings in time, and a lot more pleasure in a purchase.

20 ✔ Keep Track of Your Money

Many of us end up with too much month at the end of our paycheck. Here are some ways to track where your money is spent:

- *Set up a simple ledger system for keeping track of your money.* Include both income and expenses. An expense ledger is a "clustering" activity. Record income and expenses according to different categories of purchase. Your ledger will generally have the same categories as your budget.

- *Save every receipt and record every purchase.* If you don't get a receipt with a purchase, make a note on a scrap of paper. Periodically, record your purchases in a ledger. Divide your ledger according to categories: mortgage, food, clothing, yard care, medical, and so forth. You may have as many as twenty to thirty categories. If the purchase isn't tax deductible, or if you don't need to compare the receipt to a monthly statement, toss it after recording the amount.

  At the end of each month, tally up your

purchases in any given category and compare them to your budget. Where have you gone over or under budget? By comparing your actual expenses against your budget, you can keep your overall financial picture in order. It's easier to put on the brakes of your spending if you catch yourself speeding before going too far down the road.

- *Balance your bank accounts monthly.* Do this without fail. You'll save yourself overdraft charges, and have a feeling of greater control over your finances. If you have made a math error, it's better to catch it within a matter of days than to let it go on for months.

- *Keep a tax record box or file.* As you record your expenses, put receipts related to taxes in a separate file. Put your bank statements and completed check registers in a box; at year's end, your detailed ledger, tax file, and banking box should provide you with all of the information you need for fairly quick and easy preparation of your tax forms.

TIME CONTROL

Fifteen suggestions for making
the most of your time

21 ✔ Plan Your Day

An unplanned day isn't likely to be as productive as a planned one. And, productive days tend to be ones that give more joy and a greater sense of purpose.

Live a Day at a Time   Take each day as a separate unit. Attempt to do in a day all that you can do, and then move on to the next day. Don't live in the past, or you'll always feel as if you are playing catch-up. If you live in the future, you'll probably never arrive where or when you thought you would. Limit your scope to the sixteen or so waking hours that are immediately ahead of you.

List Tomorrow's Activities at the Close of Today   Make a list before you go to bed of all the things you want to do during the upcoming day. After listing the things you want to do, survey your list. Have you put down too many things for one day? What can you drop off the list? Don't overbook yourself.

If you could only do one thing on tomorrow's list, what would it be? Give that item the priority spot. Then rank other activities in decreasing order of importance. Consider what the optimum time for you to engage in each activity might be. Use your most productive hours for tasks that require your best effort. Schedule appointments during your less productive hours.

Identify Time Wasters   Isolate those events in your daily routine that eat up time without giving you much reward. Try to eliminate them, or cut down on their number, frequency, and time allotment. The same goes for interruptions; learn to say no to events or activities.

Schedule Alone Time   Be sure to include some time on your schedule every day in which you can be alone, to do what you want to do. You need to have a little time you can call your own— for meditation, prayer, or just a little bit of distance from the hectic swirl of the world. Your day will feel as if you have more order and balance to it if you'll schedule at least a half hour for yourself.

22 ✔ Delegate

If you find more things on a daily list than you can handle successfully, you have three choices: (1) do each task halfway (and feel frustrated, disappointed, and stressed); (2) don't do a task at all; (3) solicit help. This last is the best option, and one that actually provides an opportunity for relationships, joy, and greater balance in your life.

- *Determine precisely what it is that you want the other person to do.* The whole task? Part of the task? Intermittently? All the time? On a schedule? On a rotation with others? If you are soliciting help from a superior, be able to state why you need help and exactly what form you would like the help to take. Be able to state your request in clear, concise terms, and ask the other person to reiterate their new responsibilities to you. Ask, rather than demand.

- *How much supervision will you give the other person who is helping?* Continuous? (If so, you haven't truly delegated.) Periodic? None? Delegating doesn't mean abdicating;

it does mean that you accept ultimate responsibility for the task, but that you are giving the majority of that responsibility to another person.

All Hands on Deck   No one is too young to help around the house; have something for everybody to do. Chores shouldn't be an option for children; they should be a part of life's routine.

Keep in mind that nothing is ever done perfectly, even by you! Relax and compromise. If you don't, you probably won't enjoy the time you have freed up by delegating.

Share the Reward   You'll be gaining a reward through delegating: valuable time. Make sure the person to whom you have delegated a task is also rewarded in some way.

23 ✔ Take Time to Do It Right

A job done halfway is a job that is likely to need redoing. A job done halfheartedly is likely to be a job that brings no sense of satisfaction, fulfillment, or joy.

If you agree to undertake a task or relationship, put your best effort into it. That includes giving the task or relationship sufficient time.

Sufficient Time Sufficient time has two dimensions: quality and quantity. The quality of a time segment is usually directly related to these three factors:

- *Focus.* Is the time being devoted exclusively to one task, one person, one topic? To have quality time, you need to eliminate all distractions.

- *Shared Meaning.* All persons involved must regard the time as valuable and important.

- *Satisfaction.* When the time segment is over, all parties involved should feel a sense of satisfaction, resolve, accomplishment, forward motion, release. There should be a sense that something has been shared, enjoyed, experienced, given, or received.

The quantity of a time segment requires that you make certain you have given yourself enough time to do or contribute your best. Doing your best doesn't mean demanding perfection from yourself or others. There's a balance between attempting to do excellent work and doing perfect work. Perfection generally requires more time and money than can be regained or justified.

Time Axioms   Keep in mind these two key principles about time. *You never arrive if you don't get started.* Avoid the tendency to procrastinate. Jump into projects with both feet, and a lot of enthusiasm. The only way you can ever have sufficient time for a project is if you begin immediately; otherwise, you'll always feel behind and scrambling to make a deadline.

The longer and more frequent the time segments you allocate to something, the more you'll build momentum. Even though you may break a major project down into segments, cluster the segments together and work to build a sense of forward motion.

24 ✔ Schedule Maintenance

Every aspect of your life requires maintenance: your health, home, vehicle, relationships, career, faith, finances. To maintain involves repairing, refurbishing, replacing, restoring, renewing, realigning, rebuilding. The important news about maintenance is that it saves both time and money in the long run. The good news about maintenance is that it can be scheduled. You have control over when, where, and how maintenance takes place.

On an annual basis, schedule key maintenance days. Put them in red on a calendar and consider them appointments that can't be adjusted except in emergency situations. Include the following:

- *An annual physical exam* for yourself and for each child.

- *Annual or semiannual visits to medical specialists* who are helping you manage long-term health, such as your dentist, optometrist, dermatologist.

- *A meeting with your financial adviser, accountant, or tax attorney.* Do this at the beginning of the third quarter of your fiscal year. That way, you will still have time to make some adjustments within your fiscal year, and at the same time, get a running start on planning your financial strategy for the coming year.

- *Any meetings you anticipate needing with other key professionals, associates, or clients,* such as your attorney, stock broker, insurance agent, key staff members or colleagues, or major clients.

- *Maintenance on your heating and air conditioning units* prior to the season in which they will be needed most.

- *A maintenance-review day for your house and yard.* Are there trees that need to be trimmed or removed? Shingles that need to be replaced?

- *A time for a spiritual retreat,* perhaps a day, weekend, or week, either to be alone, with your spouse, with your family, or with others of like faith.

- *A time for a family vacation,* with major emphasis on recreation, relaxation, and renewal.

- *A time of learning, mental and creative stimulation, growth*—perhaps a short course, a special series of lectures or concerts, a set of lessons, or a seminar.

- *Vehicle maintenance.* Consult the odometer on each vehicle you own, and estimate when you will need to take the vehicle in for maintenance, as recommended in your owner's manual. Include as vehicle maintenance the renewal of licenses.

Remind Yourself to Make Appointments   Prior to key dates on your calendar, remind yourself to make appointments. For example, a couple of months prior to the date you've designated for your physical exam, write a little note on your calendar: "Call today for annual physical date. See March 23."

Keep Your Maintenance Dates   Don't shove maintenance to the side because something better or more important pops up. If you must readjust a date, make sure you don't eliminate the maintenance appointment. Reschedule it as soon as possible.

25 ✔ Hire Professionals When You Need Them

You may be *able* to do it yourself, but not want to spend the time; you may *not* be able to do it yourself. Either way, if you hire it done, choose a professional. This person has done the job before, has a track record of good performance, and is willing to supply you with references.

Check references before making a final decision. Ask if the person is willing to sign a performance agreement, a statement guaranteeing his or her work, or a document that outlines mutual expectations. A true professional will stand by his or her work.

Get an estimate. A true professional will not only be able to supply you with a written estimate or a statement of hourly fees, but will consider it a normal part of doing business. Professional help may cost a little more than doing the job yourself. But, in the long run, professional help is likely to be cost effective in terms of time.

Balancing Time and Money As you weigh the need for professional services, here are some questions to ask.

- *If I Do It.* Can I do this task? Can I do it as well as a professional? How long would it take me to do it? Will I need to buy any special tools or equipment that I don't already have? How much will my doing this disrupt our normal family routine or schedule? Will I enjoy doing it? Will my family enjoy my doing it, or enjoy helping?

- *If They Do It.* How much more will it cost for me to have this job done by a professional? Will that person be able to save me money in some way? Will they be able to do this job in a way that brings less disruption to my sense of personal or family balance?

- *Who Will Do It?* If the trade-off comes down to time or money, which would I rather have? If I choose time, will I consider the money well-spent?

26 ✔ Once-a-Month Errands

Ever hear of the days when folks only went to town once a month? That principle can still work for you, to time-saving advantage.

The Errand Basket During my growing-up years, my mother had a small basket in her home office in which she put little slips of paper, each with a specific errand or purchase that she anticipated making the next time we went to the city, which was twenty miles away. When errand day arrived, Mom went through her slips of paper, gathering together various items and sorting them geographically. Off we went. As each errand was completed, we'd tear up the slip and toss it into the litter caddy. If the errand couldn't be accomplished for some reason, we put the slip of paper to the bottom of the pile and returned it to the basket once we got home. It was a game, of sorts, for us to see what all we might accomplish in six hours of running city errands, with only one round trip's worth of gasoline and time.

I still follow that example, which I share with my own children in these words: Let's not venture out to the mall until we have sufficient reason to go.

27 ✔ Map Out Errand Runs

In gathering errands and lists together for periodic shopping excursions, you'll find that you can save a great deal of time by clustering your errands according to the following:

Geographic Location Map out a route for your errands. While in an area of town, or an area of the mall, do everything there that you need to do. If you have older children or teens who are going along, you may want to give them the challenge of figuring out the best way to go.

As you anticipate going into a well-frequented grocery or department store, map out a strategy in your own mind for getting all of the items on your list in the least amount of time. You may enjoy walking up and down each aisle occasionally, but you don't need to go up and down every aisle on every trip.

Time of Day Try to get to the busiest or most popular store on your agenda as it opens. You'll get a better parking spot, better service, and save minutes in the process. If you need to drop off an item for repair, evaluation, or processing, plan to make those stops among your first ones of the day.

End your errands and head for home before rush hour traffic; or plan to have supper out as a treat at the close of your errand run, and return home after the rush hour. Hours spent idling on a freeway are wasted.

Divide and Shop   Older children and teen-agers will enjoy having time to shop on their own. Synchronize your watches, set a meeting time and location, and go your separate ways. You might insist that your child stay within the same store, or same department, or even within sight. You might insist that your children stay together as a group. You'll all enjoy the outing, and you'll be helping to develop a sense of responsibility in your child.

Running Errands with Children   Dis-cuss with your children what you are hoping to buy or do, what it is that you are looking for, and why. Try to beat your own schedule. Laugh a lot as you go. And stop occasionally to teach your child about the objects you encounter along the way, or about how to conduct certain business transactions. The time together will become both quality and quantity time, not just errand-running time!

28 ✔ Cluster Appointments

If you are going to take part of a day off for a doctor's appointment, you might as well take the rest of the day off for an eye exam, or an appointment with your attorney. Make a personal day off really count. It may not seem like a true vacation day, but it's likely to be a satisfying day of accomplishment, a day that restores a sense of balance and control, and a day that provides a change of pace.

Choose professionals who will help you stick to your schedule. You shouldn't have to wait in a doctor's or dentist's office more than twenty minutes. If you do, talk to your physician about the wait. Ask if there's a better time of day for you to make an appointment so that you can both stay on schedule. Let the professional know that you value his or her time and expertise greatly, but that you also value your own time.

Family Appointments If you are making an appointment for your child to see the family dentist, make back-to-back appointments for all your children. Better to spend an hour at the dentist and have all three children see the dentist than to spend an hour coming and going from each of three appointments. The same can go for back-to-school physicals, eye appointments, and shoe shopping.

Group Training   If there's a new skill to be learned, gather everyone together for a one-time explanation or training session. The task need not be a major one; it might be instruction on how to use the new phone system or how to attach and use the new lawn sprinkler.

29 ✔ Use the Phone

Don't drive—dial. A phone call can accomplish a great deal. Even a brief call can help you remember a birthday or other special occasion, maintain a relationship across a great distance, get information on the price, availability, or specifications of a product, service, or event, get directions, or place an order. As an added bonus, you can shop, gather information, exchange opinions, make decisions, and conduct meetings by phone without giving a second thought to your own physical appearance.

Good Phone Use Use the phone with your intended purpose in mind. If you get a machine, leave a message. If all you intended to do with the call was convey a piece of information, don't invite a return call.

Use your own answering machine to screen calls. In your answering machine message, ask for as much information as possible. Try to avoid having to return calls only to get a needed fact or two.

Establish a Phone Time in Your Work Day

Use low-energy hours for making and returning phone calls. Invite others to call you during that same time. Let it be known that your mornings are for creative work or intense project development, and that you receive and return calls in the afternoon.

The Advantage of Portable and Speaker Phones

Cordless phones, cellular phones, and even phones with speakers or extra long cords, can give you a great deal of mobility and allow you to talk even as you engage in another activity.

30 ✔ Establish a Daily Household Routine

Put your household on a schedule and you'll not only save time, but you'll actually become more spontaneous. Here's how.

Create a Family Routine Establish a set pattern of times for going to bed and getting up. This can vary from person to person, but make certain that each person has a schedule of sleep which becomes a norm. Without sufficient regular patterns of sleep, the rest of a day's schedule is difficult to set or maintain.

Based on getting-up times and bedtimes, establish times for a family breakfast and dinner. Give yourself enough time to enjoy these meals together as a family. Even if you only carve out fifteen minutes to sit down together for each meal, you'll benefit by having this time together to share your lives, to plan your days, to discuss your tragedies, triumphs, and trials, to share opinions and insights, to exchange news, to bring up questions. Set times for:

- *Chores.* If you want the trash taken out in the morning, put it on the schedule. If you want the bed made before the child has breakfast, set up the routine that way.

- *Homework.* The time for homework may be right after school, right after dinner, or a few minutes in the morning before school. Set aside a place and time for quiet concentration.

- *Practice.* If you have more than one child needing to put in practice time on the family piano, schedule it.

- *Bathtime.* If you have more than two people sharing a bathroom, you'll need to come up with a schedule—showers in the morning for some, baths at night for others.

Where's the Spontaneity? Every hour that isn't scheduled or every minute that is created when a task is completed satisfactorily ahead of schedule becomes a moment for fun. Free time becomes the goal and the reward. This approach helps a child set priorities and become self-motivating and self-rewarding.

A family with a routine is a family that has an overall sense of order. In the process, you'll be teaching your children principles of time management that can last an entire lifetime.

31 ✔ Avoid the Crunch of Holiday Shopping

You can save a great deal of time and money by planning your gift-giving on an annual basis and making purchases all through the year. Include birthday, anniversary, and graduation gifts on your annual list.

You'll save time by avoiding holiday traffic, busy shopping centers, and long lines. You'll save money by taking advantage of sales, and by budgeting your giving dollars as a hedge against impulse buying and last-minute overspending.

Have a Gift Drawer or Trunk Have a place you can designate as a gift container, and use it for stashing gifts as you purchase them throughout the year. You can help ensure the secrecy of your gifts by wrapping them immediately after their purchase.

You will want to carry your master gift list with you at all times. Be sure to include a couple of all-purpose gifts on your annual list, such as candles, sachets, gift soaps, or specialty tea bags. That way, you'll never need to rush out for a last-minute gift. Should an unexpected guest arrive during a holiday celebration, you'll be able to present a gift with just a few minutes of preparation.

Gift-Giving Supplies   Cluster all of your gift-wrapping supplies, including wrapping and tissue paper, ribbons and bows. Buy your supplies during sales, the best of which usually occur in late December or early January.

32 ✔ Enlist Your Friends as Scouts

Do you want to locate a hard-to-find item, a certain antique pattern, a scarf or accessory with specific colors, a great buy on a specific model of appliance or piece of furniture? Ask your friends to keep their eyes open on your behalf.

Shopping Savvy You certainly can't explore every store or contact every supplier of an item in your area. And bargains and distinctive items are sometimes found in the least likely places.

Virtually everyone has at least one or more friends who love to shop. They'll probably be delighted to help you out; in fact, they'll probably find great satisfaction in looking on your behalf. (It gives them an excuse to explore new stores or to justify time spent browsing.)

Friendly Advice Sometimes friends or acquaintances are actually quite experienced or knowledgeable about a particular item. For example, you may have a friend who is a real car nut— a person who is frequently trading in cars, making deals, scouting out the showrooms, test-driving new models, talking about various vehicles.

Ask that friend's advice as you do research on the purchase of a new vehicle for yourself. They'll be able to tell you a great deal that you won't have gained from other sources. Then, if you narrow your choice to a particular model or two, you might ask the person again for their opinion, or ask where they think you can get the best price or deal.

33 ✔ Redeem the Spare Minutes

Everybody has a few spare minutes in every day. Give some order and fulfillment to this time by finding innovative uses for it.

Here are things you can do that take only a few minutes—time you might have while waiting for the children to emerge from school, for your appointment to arrive, for your plane to begin boarding:

- Write out a list

- Balance your checkbook

- Clean out your purse

- Read a passage from the Bible

- Do some isometric exercises

- Skim through a magazine, journal article, or report

- List your expenses on an expense-account form

- Memorize a verse of Scripture or the stanza of a poem

Items to Have with You Always   There are items I carry with me virtually everywhere. They all fit very easily in a briefcase or large purse or tote. As a result, I always have plenty to do, even if I only have five or ten minutes of time. These include: *my master calendar,* which includes my lists, address book, several cards with envelopes, stamps for both postcards and letters, and blank notepaper for making lists, *a purse-size copy of the Bible, my checkbook register, magazine articles,* or *a paperback book* I want to read, and *a small tape recorder and three tapes* (one of inspiration or education, one of music, and one blank, for recording my own ideas).

Information on the Go   Consider using commuting time to learn a new skill, a new language, or listen to a new novel or self-help lecture. Numerous audiocassette programs are available for check-out through public libraries. Your friends may also be willing to loan you a set of seminar tapes, a novel on tape, or other materials they have purchased or acquired. Turn your car or train into a moving continuing-education center.

Fitness for Body and Mind   You can also use a Walkman or cassette player to add to your storehouse of knowledge while you walk or jog, ride an exercise bike, or use a rowing machine.

34 ✔ Landscape with Time in Mind

Unless gardening and yard upkeep are your passions, you may find that the ground around your house yields more burden than joy. If that's the case, you have two options:

Hire It Done If you choose this route, hire reliable experts whom you don't need to supervise closely, and work out a payment plan that doesn't require your presence while the work is being done.

Simplify the Process Choose plants and trees that require minimal care. Evergreens have a lot going for them! Consider adding more beds for shrubs and flowering bushes, reducing the square yards of grass that need to be mowed, weeded, fertilized, and watered. Once planted, a bed with a few large shrubs and a thick layer of bark covering the ground requires far less care than grass.

Create patios and other areas that can be swept or washed off easily. Consider limiting your annual flowers to a few beds or pots. Choose plants that are suited for your geographic area, and that grow with minimal pruning, spraying, fertilizing, or fumigating.

If you have two green thumbs and you love to putter in the garden, if you enjoy the pleasures of home-grown vegetables, fruits, and flowers, or if you derive benefit from sweating out your frustrations as you mow the yard, then design your yard to give you the pleasures you enjoy. The time a complicated yard takes probably won't seem wasted or burdensome to you.

What goes for yards can also apply to house plants or pots of flowers and vegetables on a patio or balcony in an apartment complex. Unless you enjoy having living plants around, don't feel compelled to have them.

If you have young children, landscape with their safety in mind. Avoid using chemicals on your lawn. Don't plant bushes that produce poisonous berries. Keep areas clear for play.

35 ✔ The Night Before

Even the most energetic "morning" person should make good use of the last hour of the preceding day. During the final hour before you begin preparing for bed, make your list of things to do the upcoming day and prioritize your agenda.

Get out the garments you plan to wear, as well as the garments, socks, and shoes for each of your children. Also put out any accessories, such as belts, hair ribbons, ties, or jewelry.

Load up your briefcase or tote bag with the things you anticipate taking with you through the day. Make certain you have all of the phone numbers or addresses that you need, and any information or items that will be part of your errand-running or shopping stops.

Prepare as much as possible the things that you intend to include in a sack lunch. Sort things out for easy assembly the following morning.

As you undress, put your clothes immediately into the proper laundry hampers, and insist that your children do the same.

If you have any personal care routines, do them before you go to bed. You'll do a better job than if you try to do them as part of the morning rush.

If you need to, set two alarms—one of which is across the room.

You'll probably sleep easier knowing that you've already got a running start on the next day, and you'll be far less likely to forget something in the hurry of the next morning.

INFORMATION CONTROL

Nine quick and simple ideas
for managing the flow of communication
in your life and family

36 ✔ Mail Control

A few simple principles can help you dramatically in controlling the amount of paper you receive through the mail.

Eliminate the Junk   If you are tired of having to deal with vast amounts of junk mail, you can write: Mail Preference Service, Direct Marketing Association, 6 East 43rd Street, New York, NY 10017. They will see that your name is no longer sold to large mailing list companies. This one step alone can reduce your junk mail by nearly half.

If you order from a catalog, and the order form has a box that says, "I prefer my name not be made available for special offers of similar merchandise," check the box.

Deal with Every Piece of Mail Only Once   Immediately sort the mail as it comes in. If you can tell by the envelope that the contents are soliciting a donation or purchase, and you know you aren't interested, tear the envelope in half through your name and address and pitch it.

Put bills in a bill-paying pile to be opened and processed later.

Lay aside magazines, journals, and catalogs. Don't even open a magazine unless you plan to read or look through it thoroughly and then discard it. If you have no interest in a catalog, toss it, unopened.

Open first-class letters and business mail only when you have time to read through it fully. (You may want to stick it in your tote for reading during a spare minute of your day.)

Know When to Toss It   Throw away thank-you notes after you've read them. Don't keep birthday cards or greeting cards longer than a week. They're fun to look at, but unnecessary to store.

Discard packaging. If possible, recycle cardboard. You might want to devote a large trash bag to storing foam peanuts. Use that material, rather than newspaper, to cushion items you send.

Limit Your Subscriptions   Only subscribe to those publications you actually read. If you find an article in a magazine that you want to read, but don't have time to read it in its entirety, tear out the article and toss the rest of the magazine. If you can't seem to bear throwing out a magazine, remove your name and address from it and leave it in a laundromat or waiting room.

Don't save daily newspapers past midnight. Pitch them into a recycling bin.

As soon as you receive a catalog, toss its predecessor. As soon as you've looked through a catalog and decided against making any purchases, toss it. If you find an item you might like to purchase, tear it out, along with the order form, and put it in your to-buy file. Don't keep a catalog beyond the season of its issuance.

Develop Skimming Skills If you are a slow reader, consider taking a speed-reading course. You can save yourself lots of hours in the course of your life, and learn more at the same time.

Learn to read headlines and subheads, first paragraphs, quotes and captions, as a fast way of getting an overview.

37 ✔ Keep a Daily Set of Files

As you process mail and information on a daily basis, put items into one of these five file folders, which you may want to keep handy in your office or kitchen in a hanging file system:

The To-Do File Invitations that need a response, recipes to try, correspondence to answer —these are the types of items to put in your to-do file. Include information about movies, concerts, seminars, or other events you may want to consider attending. Also include in this file the names and addresses of places you may want to write for information. Process this file at least once a week.

The To-Pay File Bills and subscription renewal forms go here. This is also the place to put your receipts from purchases made. Deal with this file at least once a week.

The To-Buy File Clippings from catalogs, newspapers, or magazines go here. Evaluate this file at least once every few weeks. If you find that you are no longer interested in an item or an event, toss the information about it.

The To-Read File Articles, brochures, and newsletters go here—but only if you really want to read them. Carry this file with you in your briefcase, tote, or carry-on luggage. After you read an article, toss it.

The To-File File Make sure you really need to keep the information you put into this file. Certain business records and research for future projects are readily justifiable. Most information should probably be tossed, not filed. The only reason to file an item is if you anticipate you'll need to refer to the information within the next six months. If you think your reference point is likely to be longer than that—and it isn't a document you may need for tax or long-range business purposes—toss it. The information probably won't be current enough for your purposes. Discipline yourself to empty this file at least once a week.

38 ✔ Label It

Develop the habit of labeling or identifying items clearly. You'll save yourself time and frustration.

- Label the contents of boxes you store in closets, basements, or garages.

- Identify the people, places, and dates associated with photographs. Write gently with a pen on the back of the photograph or along the side of a slide. You may think now that you'll always remember the names of the people in the photograph or the year it was taken, but you won't!

- Keep a running list of the items in your gift container.

- Label and date items you put into your freezer. It's difficult to tell the difference between beef stew and chili after the concoction has been frozen for a while.

- Label all keys.

- Write your name in books you want to keep, on the inside of the front cover,

rather than on a page that might be torn out.

It only takes a few seconds to prepare and attach a label or a descriptive statement. Those few seconds can save you hours of search-and-remember time later.

39 ✔ Have One Central Message Board

Have a central place in your home where you can leave or receive messages. This family bulletin board should be located adjacent to the master family calendar. Both should be close to a phone. Make certain that pens and small pads of paper are readily accessible.

Get into the habit of putting the person's name in bold letters at the top of a message. If the message is for everybody in the family, write *everybody* or *you*.

Develop the habit of consulting the message board when you enter the house. As you leave home, develop a habit of jotting down where you have gone, what time you are leaving, when you expect to return, and how you can be reached.

Remove messages as soon as they have been received.

Keep a pen and pad of notepaper next to each phone in the house, and also by the side of your bed. That way, you'll be able to capture ideas and messages as they occur.

40 ✔ Medical Records

Medical information must be accessed quickly and thoroughly. In a time of crisis, there's no time to rummage through files. Here are six easy-to-implement suggestions that also have the potential for being life-saving ideas:

- *Post emergency first-aid information on the inside of a bathroom cabinet or cupboard.* Posters or charts are available that give quick summaries about what to do in case of burns, choking, allergic reactions, broken or sprained limbs, poisons, bleeding, fainting, muscle injuries, stings and bites. Be sure the information includes illustrated step-by-step procedures for the Heimlich technique and mouth-to-mouth resuscitation, as well as a diagram of artery pressure points.

- *Keep a simple first-aid manual clustered with your basic first-aid kit or supplies in that same cabinet.* Periodically check your first-aid kit to make certain that you have adequate supplies of tape, gauze, bandages, and other items. Keep a similar first-aid kit and manual in each of your family vehicles.

- *Keep all prescription medications clustered.* If you have young children in your home, make sure that they cannot gain access to prescription medications, or to any health-care product that might be harmful to them. Discard all out-of-date medications, empty bottles, or prescription medications that are no longer needed.

- *Carry with you at all times a list of medications that you or members of your family require.* Include the complete name of the medication, the dosage prescribed, and the prescribing physician.

- *Post the name and number of your primary-care physician on your central message board and leave it there permanently.* Teach your children how and when to use 911 to call for medical or emergency help. If 911 service is not available in your community, list the numbers to call for ambulance, fire fighting, or police assistance, and the name of your physician.

- *Develop a medical file folder for each member of your family, and keep it with your first-aid supplies and manual.* This folder should list the dates of immunizations, surgeries, and other medical procedures. It should include names and phone numbers for all physicians regularly consulted by the person. Also list any medications that are taken on a regular ongoing basis. And, make sure that the file has the name and other pertinent information related to your health insurance coverage.

Having this information handy in an emergency can help a physician in diagnosing and treating a situation promptly and effectively.

41 ✔ Information Access

There's nothing quite as frustrating as not having the information you need, when and where you need it! Here are suggestions for bringing order to information.

- *Keep an extra copy of the phone book in your car.* It will probably slide easily under the front seat. If you aren't able to get an extra copy of the current book, carry the one that just expired. Tape a couple of quarters to the inside cover of the book. That way, you'll always have change for a call.

- *Keep a detailed and up-to-date map of your city and state in each family vehicle.* Teach your children how to read a map and give clear directions.

- *Make certain the operational manual to each vehicle remains within that vehicle.* Keep maintenance records up to date.

- *Have babysitter information clearly spelled out and made readily available.* Go over it with your sitter before you leave. Don't assume the sitter will find it or read it on her own. Be sure to leave clear instructions about what you expect the sitter to do. Tell where you have gone, when you expect to return, and how you can be reached. Show the sitter the name and address of your family physician. Show the sitter where you have put the medical files, emergency medical information, and first-aid kit. Give precise instructions about what you want the sitter to do if you cannot be reached.

- *Keep a record of the sizes worn by every member of your family at any given time.* Carry it with you among your lists. You'll save lots of time in exchanging clothing.

- *Cluster all warranties and operations manuals* for your currently owned appliances and equipment.

- *Carry your date book, address book, and lists with you at all times.*

42 ✔ Permanent Records

Here is information you should keep, and update periodically, as part of a permanent record of your life.

A Perpetual Calendar Invest in a perpetual calendar, a date book that gives dates but not days or years. Use this calendar to record births, anniversaries, graduations, baptisms, dates of death, and key dates in your business life.

A Gift Record Purchase a blank book in which you can record—by person—the gifts you have given and received. How many times have you purchased multiple items on a trip, only to forget to whom you gave them? A perpetual gift record can answer the question for you within seconds.

Holiday Card List You may find it useful to keep track of those with whom you have exchanged greeting cards through the years. You may want to indicate whether your relationship to the person is a business or personal one.

Entertainment Records You may find it helpful to record menus and guest lists for specific parties or events.

A Master Address Book You probably don't need or want to carry with you all of the names and addresses of people you have met, done business with, or are related to. One of the best ways to keep a master address file is to put the addresses on 3"×5" cards. That way, the names are easily alphabetized, the file is readily expanded, and you'll also have room for making notes related to the person (food allergies or preferences, names of nearest relatives, or name of employer). Date the card, so that you have a record of how current the information is. Use pencil rather than ink so you can update addresses and phone numbers.

A Job Diary You will probably benefit by having some record of when certain business transactions were conducted, projects were begun or completed, contracts were signed, items were shipped, and so forth. You can construct a job diary by taking a couple of minutes at the close of each work day and writing on your master calendar major transactions or work accomplished.

A Personal Journal Keeping a personal journal is an excellent way of recording the key events of your personal life and of gaining a perspective about yourself over time. Make regular entries. Note your feelings, the highlights of important conversations, your observations, and your opinions, as well as the facts about what you have done and where you have gone.

These permanent documents of your life will become your memory, and they will also give your heirs or survivors interesting insights into your life. Consider them to be historical documents. Be accurate and as complete as possible in your entries.

43 ✔ Purge Your Papers

Just as there are some documents and records worth keeping, there are others that should be discarded when their usefulness has expired.

Out-of-Date Information If information is no longer current, get rid of it. If you find warranties, operations manuals, or invoices related to items you no longer possess, discard them.

Old Files and Records Cluster vital business documents together. Chances are, the truly important business documents in your life (deeds, copies of your will, information about bank accounts, final wishes, policy numbers) can be kept in one expanding file. Consult your accountant or tax attorney for advice on how long you need to keep other business files and tax-related documents. Label your boxes or containers of business documents by year, and when you've passed the recommended time limit for keeping the documents, discard them!

Purge your file cabinets at least twice a year. If you haven't needed the information for the past six months, you are probably never going to need it.

Reevaluate Your Library Do you derive pleasure from having books around? Do you need books for research? Fine. But if books are taking up space you'd rather use for something else, start a give-away program. Contribute your unwanted books to a local school or charity that sponsors an annual book fair, or donate your books to a library, secondhand store, or senior citizens' center. The same goes for back issues of magazines.

Reevaluate your music, audiotape, and video-tape libraries. Share information and music. Unless you're certain you want to keep an item for future reference or as a lasting reminder of your youth, pass it along to someone else who might benefit from it or find pleasure in it.

44 ✔ Simple Lend-and-Return Strategies

If you have items you don't mind loaning to others but you want returned, it will be up to you to make certain that you set up the best possible system for ensuring that the loaned items find their way home.

Identify Your Ownership of Books, Videos, Games, Tapes, and CDs Find a style of bookplate you like and invest in a large quantity of them. Affix them to the inside front cover of books, on videotapes you own (on the tape itself, not the box), on the back of audiotapes and game boards, on the inside front or back of CD holders. The first step in getting items returned is to let a person know clearly, at a glance, that the item is yours.

Keep a Check-Out Record You might want to keep a blank book in an accessible place so you can record the loan of a particular item. You don't need to call attention to the book or make a formal ceremony out of lending an item. Simply jot a line to yourself after loaning an item you want to see again. If the item is not returned in a timely fashion, you'll remember whom you need to call.

State Your Desire to Have the Item Returned
When you loan an item, state clearly, "I'd appreciate your returning this when you are finished with it. That way I can loan it to another friend in the future."

Potluck ID
When taking a dish to a group picnic, company party, or potluck dinner, be sure to label your container. Put your name on a bit of masking tape and attach it to the bottom of the dish so you can identify it later. Avoid taking your best china, silver, or sterling flatware.

Sharing with Roommates
Have a clear-cut agreement with any roommate about what is yours and what isn't, as well as what you are making available for communal use and what is for your own private use. Avoid purchasing items together. If you do purchase a lasting item that is for mutual use and enjoyment, such as a piece of furniture, appliance, or decorative item, keep a record of your purchase and date it.

LIFE SIMPLIFIERS

Seven strategies for
simplifying your everyday life

45 ✔ Limit the Traffic

Your home doesn't need to be Grand Central Station. Let others in your circle of friends, and your children's friends, share the responsibility for hosting, entertaining, and child-watching.

- *Limit the meetings.* Put a limit on the number of nights a month that you have meetings, groups, or parties in your home.

- *Limit the number of dinner guests.* Consider having only one night a week or one meal a week when you have a guest for dinner. Rotate the choice of guest among household members.

- *Limit the number of friends who come over.* More than two friends per child and you tend to end up with a party or a war. Take turns having friends over.

- *Limit heavy traffic to certain rooms in the house.* Keep children confined to a child's bedroom or playroom. Keep food and beverage consumption confined to the kitchen or outdoors.

- *Limit the number of sleep-over nights your children host* to an occasional guest or a once-a-year party. You don't need to host friends every weekend.

- *Limit access to your yard,* especially your swimming pool, outdoor gym equipment, or any athletic courts. You may be held legally and financially responsible for any accidents that occur in your yard or home. Make sure your insurance coverage is adequate. Insist that guests use your yard and pool only when you are present or on invitation.

Limit; Do Not Eliminate By limiting the traffic in your home, you are not necessarily eliminating people from your life or diminishing relationships. If your friends, or your children's friends, only like you because of your ability to entertain, they aren't true friends.

Limiting the level of traffic through your home cuts down on expense, frees up more of your time, lessens the wear and tear on your furniture and yard, and adds a greater feeling of peace and tranquility to your home. It's a compliment, of course, to have everyone want to meet at your house. Remain a gracious hostess—less frequently.

Limit Your Own Goings and Comings

Even as you cut back on the number of people who come into and through your home, attempt to limit the number of trips you need to make to and from your house. Run errands and make shopping stops en route to and from work or meetings. Share carpooling responsibilities with others. Use home-delivery services. You'll streamline the use of your time, spend less money in vehicle use, and probably feel a greater sense of order in your life.

46 ✔ Streamlining the Cleanup

Washing and cleaning up can seem like endless activities. The key principle to remember is that everyone does their share.

- *Everyone clears their own place at the table and rinses off the dishes.* Teach your children how to load and run the dishwasher. If you don't have a dishwasher, consider getting one. Until you get one, include your children in the wash-and-dry process.

- *Everyone puts their clothes into laundry hampers at the end of the day.* You can facilitate the laundry process by using multiple laundry hampers: one for whites, one for delicates, one for colored clothes. Stackable bins can make the sorting easy. Even young children can sort. And, if everyone pitches in—and pitches their clothes into the right bins—the laundry gets done much faster.

  Everyone should be able to do a load of laundry. Post very simple instructions for washing clothes in a visible place near your washing machine and dryer. Teach your children how to load the machine and run it, how to measure detergents and use fabric softeners. Teach your children how to sort out garments that do not go in the dryer, and how to hang garments on a clothesline. Let everybody, even your three-year-old, help fold towels and sheets.

- *Everyone makes their own bed, empties their own wastepaper basket, hangs up their own clothes, folds their own towels on the rack in the bathroom, and picks up their own room.* Children older than six can help in the cleaning process, learning to vacuum, dust, mop, and clean windows. Children older than eight should be taught to use an iron.

- *Everyone has "family help" chores.* It may be as simple as bringing in the paper and mail, taking out the trash, setting the table, raking leaves, sweeping off the porch.

Make the Most of Machines

Let machines work for you. Don't have what you don't need, but *DO* have what helps.

If you are in the market for a stove, get one with a self-cleaning oven. If you are in the market for a new refrigerator, get one that you don't need to defrost. If you need a lawn mower, consider one of the new models that mulches, and is self-propelling. Consider getting a dishwasher and a trash compactor.

Good Cleanup Gear and Clothing Invest in a good mop, a good ceiling brush, and good brooms. Have the brushes, pails, and scrubbers you need. Wear gloves when gardening or cleaning. Wear goggles or dust masks when you need to. When working in the yard, wear sturdy shoes and long pants. You may want to have a set of work clothes set aside for especially messy jobs.

47 ✔ Simplify Your Personal Care

Here are ways you can simplify your own personal care routines and possessions to save time, money, and inconvenience:

- *Nails.* Keep your nails short. Wear clear nail polish or buff your nails.

- *Hair.* Invest in a good haircut, and a perm if you need extra body. Choose a hairstyle that's simple to do and requires minimal fuss on your part. Cut down on the use of aerosol sprays. Your lungs, and the environment, will both benefit.

- *Carry-along supplies.* Carry duplicate containers of the beauty supplies you need in your carry-on bag, purse, or tote.

- *Don't self-prescribe.* If you develop skin problems, see a dermatologist. If you have questions about makeup, consult a makeup stylist at a department store or salon. If you have hair problems, talk to your hair stylist about them.

- *Use what works for you.* When you find a product that works for you, whether shampoo, deodorant, mascara, or razor blade, stick with it.

- *Gentle does it.* If you have sensitive skin, avoid deodorant soaps and highly perfumed products. Try hypoallergenic cosmetics.

- *Simple works.* Plain Ivory Soap and water work for most people as a way to cleanse and moisturize. Vaseline is still a highly rated skin protector. A mixture of baking soda and salt still makes an excellent toothpaste.

- *Good scents.* Find a classic fragrance that you love, and that loves you, and stay with it. Use unscented deodorants, hair sprays, and soaps. Don't confuse the aroma around you.

- *Mix and match.* Develop a wardrobe that has lots of mix-and-match separates: blazers, skirts, pants, blouses. Choose simply cut designs, solid colors, and classic weaves. You'll save yourself lots of money, and also find you have more versatility in looks for your dollar spent, less luggage to haul around on trips, a greater ability to go from dawn to midnight with just a change of accessories, and a better sense of style.

- *Lingerie.* Have enough underwear, nightwear, and hosiery to make it through a week. Always use the gentle cycle and low heat for items that have elastic or lace.

- *Shoes.* Buy only those that fit well and are comfortable the first time you put them on. Don't buy shoes with the intent of breaking them in; they usually break you first. Keep your shoes in good repair, replacing heels as you need to. Keep your shoes polished. Choose simple classic styles and low heels. They not only wear well, but they are better for your feet and back.

- *Accessories.* Become a master at accessories. They can update a wardrobe for a fraction of the cost of a new garment. Keep your jewelry simple and minimal; it will be more versatile that way.

- *Purses and wallets.* Choose ones of good quality leather, a size and style you are comfortable with, and stick with neutral colors.

48 ✔ Travel Light

Simplify your travel routines and you'll probably enjoy travel more, even boring business trips.

Carry It On Carry on everything, if you can; you'll save lots of airport time. Travel light; don't take one ounce with you that you don't absolutely need. Keep your carry-on pieces to a minimum. The more pieces you juggle, the greater the likelihood that you'll leave something behind.

If you do check your luggage, make sure you have a change of clothes with you in your carry-on bag, as well as necessary personal-care products.

Travel Sizes Use travel sizes of beauty products, or invest in small travel containers and fill them with your choice of products.

Coordinated Looks Having a mix-and-match wardrobe will be a blessing if you are going to be away more than a day or two. Switch your blouse and scarf, jewelry and belt, and nobody will notice that you wore the same pants or skirt the day before.

Wrinkle-free Choose garments that resist wrinkles. Most hotels have irons and ironing boards that you can request from housekeeping, or ask the hotel valet to press a garment for you. It costs a little but saves you time and the effort of lugging around an iron.

Worry-free   Leave cash and valuables at home.

Prepacking If you take more than one trip per month, keep a complete set of personal-care products in your suitcase at all times, along with a travel alarm clock. Keep a master list of "things to remember to take" tucked in your suitcase. It will save you hours of packing time, and you'll forget fewer necessities.

The night before, pack virtually all that you are going to take with you. If you are leaving on a family vacation by car, load up the car the night before. It you're traveling by plane, have your suitcases loaded and waiting by the front door before you go to bed, along with your tickets.

As You Go Take along a few plastic bags for storing garments that need laundering. Use shoe protectors. Have any major purchases shipped home.

49 ✔ Entertain with Ease

Think "simple and elegant" when it comes to entertaining.

Food Serve foods that are easy to prepare, easy to serve, easy to eat, and easy to clean off the carpet. Don't overload the menu; a few well-prepared items will suffice. Choose items you can prepare in advance. Get out of the kitchen and enjoy your own party!

Let others help. Barbecues are a great idea. Let some of the guests do the outside cooking while others do the inside preparation.

Encourage potlucks, with each person bringing a dish or beverage.

Decorations Use your own linens and objects you already own. Cut a few branches of greenery from your yard if you feel the need for a centerpiece of some kind.

Consider investing in clear glass dishes. Used with colorful placemats and napkins, they give you versatility in entertaining. Put a paper doily on a clear dish and you have a party platter for cookies or finger sandwiches. Slide a pewter or brass plate liner under a clear plate and you have instant elegance. Plus, they go through the dishwasher without any problem.

A Quick-Fix Party Shelf Keep a few items on hand in a cupboard for drop-in, quick-fix entertaining. A few cans or jars (salmon, tuna, smoked oysters, nuts), a few unopened boxes (specialty crackers, pasta), several bags of popcorn, a few pouches of dried fruit, an extra jar of peanut butter and jelly, and chances are, you have all that you need to throw together a light meal or quick snack for guests of any age.

Anticipate Spills and Spots Use tablecloths. Have sufficient coasters available. Hand a person a napkin as you offer a beverage or food.

Back-to-Back Parties Cluster your entertaining. Make double the amount you need, and entertain different groups of guests two days in a row.

Go Out If you really don't enjoy entertaining at home, go out instead!

50 ✔ Always with You

In addition to the money, licenses, credit cards, keys, and personal-care products most people carry with them as routine, here are a few items that you are wise to carry with you in your purse, briefcase, or tote:

- A pocket-sized calculator.

- Change for a pay phone.

- A few postage stamps.

- A small notepad of blank paper and a couple of pens.

- A small repair kit that includes several safety pins of different sizes, a needle and a few lengths of thread in basic colors, and several bandages of different sizes.

- A clean handkerchief.

- A day's supply of the medications you need, in case you don't get back home in time.

- Your planning diary or master calendar, address book, lists, and claim checks.

- A small pocket knife.

If you are traveling through life with young children, you'll obviously need to have a few other items with you at all times. One of the most valuable is a dry set of clothes carried in the trunk of your car, including underwear, socks, and shoes.

51 ✔ Build Strong and Joyous Friendships

Choose to build strong and joyous friendships. In order to do that, you will need to limit your associations. In so doing, you'll also be limiting your obligations and responsibilities.

You simply cannot be a close friend to everybody. Friendships take time to build and sustain. In fact, you probably can't develop, successfully, more than a dozen close friendships. Having four or five close friends is more likely. Having even one close friend is a blessing!

Don't feel a need to socialize with people because you work with them, or worship with them. Choose to build friendships with people you truly enjoy being with. Cultivate these relationships. Nurture them. Find innovative and creative ways of helping them, blessing them, encouraging them. Give to them. Be there for your friends in times of crisis, in ways that are meaningful to them. And learn to receive from your friends.

What does all of this have to do with an ordered life? It has to do with balance, fulfillment, and joy.

Build friendships that are mutually supportive,

marked by open communication, trust, and laughter.

There's nothing that gives more joy to life than a long-lasting, mutually rewarding, enriching friendship. Order your life to include friends as a top priority!

II. Make Your House Look Great

✳ Contents

1 * Buy the Best Durable Goods You Can Afford

When it comes to making your house look great with a minimum of time and effort, quality is important. Durable goods are those items that are expected to last three years or longer. Whenever you make a purchase for your household that you expect to keep three years or longer, shop for quality rather than for a bargain. In the long run, you will not only save time and effort taking care of the durable goods you buy, you will actually save money. High-quality items last longer, look better, require less maintenance, and need to be replaced less often than second-rate replicas. Here are some of the items in your home for which quality is important:

- *Furniture.* High-quality furniture will last longer, wear better, and maintain a good appearance over time. If you buy cheap furniture, even if it looks great initially, inferior materials will cause the furniture not to wear well. Look for natural woods, sturdy construction, quality fabrics, and classic styles.

- *Vacuum cleaner.* Your vacuum is one of the most valuable tools you have to keep your home looking great. If you invest in a vacuum that is powerful and efficient, you will find that your carpets not only look great but last longer. Make sure your vacuum is easy to use (including the attachments) so that you will not dread using it. Check to make sure you can easily change the bag and perform routine maintenance. There are many varieties on the market, including vacuuming systems you can build into your home. Whatever vacuum you choose, don't scrimp!

- *Major appliances.* Your appliances not only perform valuable functions within your home that save you time and effort, they are also decorator items. Look for the features that best serve your family's needs, a good warranty, a quality brand name that you trust, and attractive appearance.

- *Carpet and floor coverings.* Your selection of carpet is going to make a world of difference in terms of how your house looks and how much work is required to keep your home looking great. Take care to select the best quality padding and highest grade of carpet you can afford, and make sure it is installed properly. Medium pile in a neutral tone (neither dark nor light) wears the best and is least likely to show dirt. If you scrimp on your padding or carpet quality, it will soon become apparent by worn spots in major traffic patterns of your home.

  If you rent or have carpet that doesn't look great at the moment, you can still purchase quality area rugs that will provide beauty, warmth, and comfort to your home. When you purchase floor coverings, make sure you get the best low-maintenance floor coverings available. If you want wood floors, make sure they are treated with polyurethane, which practically eliminates the work of keeping them gleaming.

2 ✻ Turn Eyesores into Pleasant Views

Every house seems to have one or two eyesores, those trouble spots that never look nice, usually because of constant use. You can use your creativity to address problem areas.

First you must take an objective look at your house with an eye for the trouble spots. Identify the eyesores and the function those spots serve. Then use your creativity to find ways to keep the functions beautifully. Here are a few ideas:

- If you use powdered laundry detergent, instead of keeping unsightly boxes sitting out, transfer the detergent and a scoop into a large decorative canister. You can keep a bouquet of silk flowers tucked in the canister when not using the detergent. Hide boxes of fabric softener sheets in pretty baskets.

- During months when the fireplace is not in use, tie logs with decorative ribbon or fill the fireplace with pine cones. Pine cones can turn a sooty fireplace into an attractive centerpiece and provide fuel for the first fire of the coming winter season. Or use a fireplace fan to cover the open fireplace entirely.

- Covered baskets create a lovely look while providing a functional way to contain small collections of items that get scattered around a room. Decorative baskets can collect hair accessories, costume jewelry, a bag of birdseed for a beloved (but messy) pet, socks, a collection of rocks, baseball cards, plastic dinosaurs, small cars, marbles, and other treasures. In a baby's room, a large wicker basket with lid can replace stacks of disposable diapers in plastic wrap. Knitting materials can be kept in painted pottery or an antique can. You may want to convert this cover-up into useful service by placing a colorful pillow on top, making the container into a stool.

- If your kitchen is cluttered with pots and pans, assortments of utensils, and foodstuffs essential to meal preparation, make these necessities part of your decorating scheme. Hang pots and pans from ceiling racks with charming effect. Use wire hanging baskets to hold colorful fruits and vegetables. A braid of garlic can liven up your kitchen decor while awaiting the time it will liven up your favorite meal.

- If cosmetics make you beautiful but make a mess of your bathroom or bedroom, create a pretty place for them. Painted porcelain bowls can hold small items. Short vases can keep eyeliner pencils or tubes of cosmetics. Or try a cosmetic organizer to make your beauty items beautiful to behold.

- If you accumulate magazines and hate to part with them, don't just leave them piled around the house while you try to curb your tendency to hold on to them. Use magazine racks or decorative tables with storage compartments where magazines can be easily accessible but out of sight.

3 ✳ Make a Game of It!

Mary Poppins is the master of this trick with her game of "Let's tidy up the nursery." In playing this game she taught little Jane and Michael that "for every job that must be done there is an element of fun; find the fun and—snap —the job's a game." Whenever the family has chores to do together, find ways to turn those mundane tasks into a challenge. Here are some ideas for how you can make a game of cleaning house:

- Group competition against the clock. Set a time limit to complete a specific goal, divide the tasks according to age and ability, name a prize for the family to share if you can beat the clock, and go for it. If one person finishes his task he may even be inspired to help in another person's area. If someone is sloughing off and not participating, peer pressure from the group will keep you from having to be the only one doing the nagging.

- Once you have taught each family member how to do the basic routines to keep your house clean (we will cover these later), set par times for completing each task. For example: daily cleaning of bathroom par—five minutes. Make a checklist for what has to be done to complete the job. Then have races to

establish new family records for each room. Keep
family record times posted, giving recognition and
small awards for the family record holder for each
particular room. Be sure judging is objective and
fair: nothing sours the competitive spirit more
quickly than feeling cheated by the judges. Younger
children who want to compete can do so with older
siblings or be given a handicap to even out their
chances.

- Race the clock by yourself. Try to estimate how
  long it will take you to perform a particular task.
  Then give yourself some small promise of a prize if
  you can finish the task within the estimated time.
  Try to challenge yourself by allowing just a little
  less time than you anticipate. Reward yourself with
  some small favor, fifteen minutes to put your feet
  up, a bubble bath, a cup of tea, or an evening walk.

- Place a basketball hoop over the hamper and score
  points for every pair of socks (folded or tied together) that make it into the hamper. Keep a plastic
  scoreboard in the room along with a dry-erase
  marker.

- Give prizes and recognition to family members who
  come up with good ideas of how to help keep the
  house looking great. At family meetings, bring up
  specific problem areas regarding housekeeping and
  allow family members to brainstorm about possible
  solutions. If an idea works, reward the contributor.
  Remember, when asking for input of this kind,
  there are no wrong answers. Always praise each
  person for her or his contribution even if it is not

entirely effective, and do not allow ridicule from other family members.

- Hold a competition every three months to see who can eliminate the most clutter or unused items from his or her personal living space and belongings. Make this a time to clean out drawers and to give away outgrown clothing and toys that no one plays with regularly. Give prizes for the person who gives away the most, the person whose room looks the most orderly after the competition, and the person who makes the greatest improvement from previous competitions.

4 ✳ Give Yourself the Right Tools and Supplies

Having the proper tools to do the job, kept in a handy spot, is one key to keeping your house looking great. It's just human nature that if you have to spend time and energy looking for the things you need to do the job you probably won't invest the extra effort. Having everything you need in one place makes the job go faster and allows you to delegate chores to others without having to take time to assemble the items they need. For these reasons it is worthwhile to keep a caddie with all necessary tools and cleaning solutions in each area where routine cleaning jobs are done and to make sure your home is well stocked with the basics necessary to keep it looking great on a regular basis.

Here are some guidelines for basics to keep in each area:

- *Bathroom:* Roll of paper towels, bowl cleaner, bowl brush, sponges, all-purpose disinfectant cleaner, glass cleaner (use glass cleaner rather than all-purpose cleaner on glass and mirrors), hamper, and wastebasket. (You may want to have complete cleaning kits for each bathroom even though they duplicate one another.)

- *Kitchen:* Paper towels, sponges, all-purpose disinfectant cleaner, powdered cleanser, dishwashing supplies, electric broom, mop, rubber gloves, glass cleaner, garbage disposal, and wastebasket.

- *Living room:* Dust cloth, dust mop (for reaching high spots), spray dusting cleaner, vacuum with accessories, glass cleaner, paper towels, wastebasket for each room or work area (if there is a desk in one corner of the living area, it should have its own wastebasket so that trash doesn't collect because the users don't want to get up to discard their trash).

- *Other basics:* Mini-vac, broom and dust pan, yard grooming equipment, household tool chest (containing hammer, nails, standard and Phillips screwdrivers, screws, pliers, wrench set, nuts and bolts, washers, thumbtacks, tape, and picture hangers), extra light bulbs, step stool, flashlight, something to remove cobwebs, ladder, and shovel.

5 * Learn to Delegate Successfully

One skill all efficient managers possess is the ability to delegate successfully. Webster's dictionary defines the verb delegate as "to entrust to another." Are you holding on to jobs you don't have time to do consistently because you believe "If I want it done right I have to do it myself"? If so, you need to learn to delegate.

Learning to delegate is easy if you commit yourself to the task. Initially it will require you (or whoever is carrying more than her fair share of the work) to become the teacher.

Follow this four-step plan for successful delegation:

1. You do the job and have them watch, as you explain the task. Have them make a checklist of all the small tasks included in completing the job while they watch you.

2. You do the job and have them help you, instructing them as they try each small task necessary for doing a complete job.

3. Have them do the job and you help them, explaining where they need to make changes in what they are doing (but not doing anything yourself).

4. Have them do the job on their own (following the checklist) while you do something else. Check their work when they think they are finished and make corrections. Be sure to praise what they did right before pointing out what is lacking.

Here are some tips for successful delegation:

- Treat delegation of household duties as an investment. If you take the time to teach others what you expect, then inspect to hold them accountable for doing the job as you have taught them, you will soon be able to entrust the job to them fully. Your initial investment of time will be rewarded when you are able to release that particular job to others.

- Call their bluff. If your family knows how difficult it is for you to let a job be done less than perfectly, they may pretend not to be able to do the job well, in hopes that you will give in and resume responsibility for the job. Don't do it! Let them know that once you have taught them how to do something within their ability you will not step in to do it for them.

- Plan and assign responsibilities well in advance to allow others to fit the delegated task into their mental plans for themselves. Don't pile work on just because you are in the mood or under pressure, running roughshod over their plans and expectations.

- Hire help when necessary. There are services available to take on almost any household task imaginable. When your family is short on time and energy, but you have room in your budget, hire the help you need.

6 * Don't Overcommit Your Time

Overcommitment is the death of order. Whenever you make commitments that exceed what you can actually do in a given day, week, month, or year, something has to be compromised. When your time is overcommitted you will find your systems break down, you get behind, laundry piles up, and work is put off until you have time for it. The job becomes bigger than if you had planned enough time to do the work on a regular schedule.

Many times keeping your house in order is what loses out because other commitments seem more pressing. The commitments you make at work, school, church, within your community, and to your friends may get priority because they involve others who don't know you well and whom you don't want to inconvenience. Even though your family members are the most important people in your life, you may allow their lives to be inconvenienced whenever you overcommit your time. Being overcommitted is also very stressful. Not only will your schedule and plans suffer, you will probably become more irritable about the things you need to do to keep your house in order.

Here are some tips to keep you from overcommitting your time:

- Never say yes automatically when asked for help. There are some people who just can't seem to say no. They gain a reputation for being helpers and are put on everyone's volunteer list. If you have this tendency, deal with it. If you can't bring yourself to say no immediately, practice saying, "Let me check my calendar and get back to you." Then check to see if you can realistically say yes without compromising the things you need to do for yourself (including keeping your house in order).

- Keep a calendar and make sure every commitment is down in writing.

- Overestimate how long things will take. Give yourself up to double the amount of time you suppose for any given task or errand. Be sure to estimate travel time, finding parking, and so on whenever you consider adding an appointment to your schedule.

- Don't pack your schedule full of productive things. Everyone needs a little space and rest. Whether you plan for it or not, you will probably end up giving yourself the rest and recreation you need. Plan some time for rest and refreshing into each day and week.

- Go over your schedule with another family member or member of your household. Take time before beginning each week to review your commitments. Allow the other person to give you feedback from his objective point of view. If it seems you have overcommitted yourself, reschedule some

things before the appointed time. In this way
you can make sure you have time to keep your
house looking great and your nerves from being
frazzled!

7 * Never Retrace Your Steps

One rule of thumb practiced and praised almost universally by professional housecleaners and successful homemakers is never to retrace your steps. Those who make a practice of this insist it cuts their work considerably. However, it does require planning and preparation. This simple change of procedure can lighten your load. Here are some ways you can plan never to retrace your steps:

- Take a bag with you as you clean and collect items that belong in another room instead of putting each item in its place as you come across it. In this way you can deliver items to their place as you arrive in each room.

- For multilevel homes, keep a basket or bag near the stairs to collect anything that needs to go to another level, then make one trip up or down the stairs when going that direction to return items to their proper places.

- When mopping, use two buckets, one filled with cleaning solution and another with rinse water. This prevents you from redistributing the dirt you've collected while mopping.

- If you iron as you do laundry, remove items to be ironed from the dryer while they are still slightly damp. In this way you avoid having to sprinkle or steam clothes after they have dried and save yourself the trouble of removing wrinkles that didn't need to be there in the first place.

- Fold or hang up everything as it comes out of the dryer to avoid having to wash and/or dry it over again. If you do happen to let clothes wrinkle in the dryer, don't iron the wrinkles out of wash-and-wear clothing. Just put a damp towel in with the dry clothes and run the dryer again.

- Wear a cleaning apron that has plenty of pockets to carry all necessary cleaning cloths, spray cleaners, and other supplies. Keep some pockets empty to allow you to carry trash and small items to their appropriate place.

- Clean mirrors, glass, and furniture from top to bottom.

- Clean through a room systematically: from left to right, right to left, or in a circle around the room.

- When leaving the bathroom after a shower or bath, clean on your way out. Start in the shower or tub. If you have glass doors, keep a squeegee and some glass cleaner on hand. Spray the doors, wipe them with the squeegee, and dry them with a paper towel. Wipe shower walls and fixtures with a towel kept in reach for this purpose. This will keep mildew and hard water spots from forming and requiring considerable scrubbing. After baths, wipe the tub dry so that a bathtub ring never has a chance to form. Have children place all bath toys in a mesh bag, and hang it on a hook or on the shower head. Hang towels on racks. If the floor is wet, wipe it with the bath mat and carry the mat to the laundry upon leaving the bathroom.

8 ✳ Revise Traditional Standards

Tradition can have a powerful influence over the way you do things, including how you go about keeping house. Tradition is fine when it serves the needs of your family or when it preserves important family values for the next generation. However, mindlessly doing something the way Mother taught you when the reason she did it in that particular way is no longer valid is a waste of time. You can hold onto precious family traditions, including keeping a clean and orderly home, without having to use your mother's antiquated methods.

Before revising your traditional standards, consider this: your mother probably had reasons for the way she did things that fit with her lifestyle. Face it—the lifestyles of women in this generation are markedly different from those of your mother's and your grandmother's generations. Today's society sees most women working to provide some portion of the family income, many women holding political office and professional positions, more divorce and single-parent families, more women completing higher education, more men sharing in the responsibilities of managing the home, more technologically advanced devices that speed up the pace of life, couples starting families at a later age, and so on. You need a housekeeping strategy that takes your lifestyle into consideration.

You have time- and energy-saving devices available to make keeping house easier than it was for your mother. She may have prided herself on waxing the floor by hand, but today you may get the same effect without the same kind of effort.

Here are some ways to revise your traditional standards:

- Reconsider everything you do a certain way just because your mother did it that way, adapting only the methods that fit your lifestyle and using the modern tools you have available to you.

- Consider allowing yourself a more relaxed standard of cleanliness, given your other commitments outside the home and how much your home is used for entertaining.

- Consider relaxing your standards for a season— while you have two little ones in diapers, while getting your doctoral degree, or while chauffeuring an assortment of children to Little League, play rehearsal, and ballet lessons.

- Always ask yourself why. Why does this have to be done on this day, in this way, this often? Why does this have to be done at all? You may discover some flexibility that helps you make your life simpler.

- Consider the purpose or effect of the traditions you follow. Try to identify what you hold dear about your traditional way of doing a particular task. Then look for a way to achieve the same effect and to preserve what you hold dear with less time and effort.

9 * Use Small Amounts of Free Time

One simple way to keep your house looking great is to practice using small amounts of time to whittle away at small jobs. Doing this consistently amounts to tackling big jobs before they become overwhelming. To do this you must learn to think of every job in its most basic parts. Instead of thinking, "I don't have time to clean the kitchen," mentally define cleaning the kitchen as several small jobs: clearing the table; rinsing dishes; unloading or loading the dishwasher; washing, drying, or putting away dishes; clearing a countertop; wiping the stove; wiping appliances; sweeping.

When you think of every job as a group of small jobs you can do something with whatever small amount of time and energy you have. You may find that breaking big jobs down this way makes the work seem more approachable and cuts down on procrastination.

Here are some ways to practice using small amounts of time to do small jobs:

- While waiting on hold on the telephone, race to see if you can clean out a drawer, clean off a countertop, or write a note before your call is attended to.

- While waiting for other family members to get ready to go, empty the dishwasher or clean out the car.

• Turn commercial time into clean-up time. While watching television, plan to use each commercial break to accomplish some small task. The time limit helps motivate making a quick job of something you might otherwise dawdle over. By the end of an hour program you will have accomplished quite a bit. If you train your entire family to do this (occasionally) while watching TV together, you will be amazed at how much you can get done during time that is otherwise wasted.

• Do what you can when you can. Keep correspondence and note cards in your briefcase or purse and write notes while waiting for an appointment.

10 * Keep Your Bathroom Clean in Five Minutes a Day

Your bathroom must be kept clean on a regular basis for sanitary reasons and because it will be seen by family members and guests alike. The bathroom is the one room in your house where people spend time in privacy, and some people just can't resist the urge to snoop! Therefore, your bathroom is one place in your home that needs to be cleaned thoroughly and regularly. The bathroom is also often the most dreaded room in the house when it comes to the thought of keeping it clean. You can keep your bathroom clean on an everyday basis (which will reduce the dread of a messy job considerably) if you practice a daily cleaning routine. This should take less than five minutes, some cleaning experts say less than three minutes. Here's how:

- Stock each bathroom with a spray bottle of disinfectant, a clean cloth, sponges, paper towels, bowl brush, toilet bowl cleaner, glass cleaner, hamper, and wastebasket.

- Teach each family member to wipe down the shower and tub quickly after each use with a towel kept in the room expressly for that purpose. (Don't have them use their towels unless they have already been used twice. This cuts down on unnecessary laundry.)

- Spray countertops, outside of toilet, and fixtures with disinfectant cleaner and wipe with a damp cloth. Work from top to bottom of the room to avoid spreading germs to the faucet handles. Wipe the toilet last.

- Swish the toilet bowl with disinfectant or bowl cleaner and brush. Allow the water to remain until next use.

- Make sure you have enough towel racks so it is easy for family members to keep their towels off the floor.

- Straighten towels and the floor mat.

- Throw away used paper towels and carry out the garbage liner with you. Hint: Keep extra trash can liners in the bottom of the trash receptacle so they are handy and can be pulled up immediately without having to come back with a fresh bag.

Once this routine becomes a family habit you will never again have to worry that your bathroom won't be presentable for guests, even if they are unexpected.

To make your job even easier, get rid of messy bar soap entirely. Switch to liquid soap in pump containers. These containers are available in a variety of lovely decorator styles. They are plastic, so there is no danger of breaking them. And they are refillable, which makes them economical. One word of warning: children tend to have fun pumping out liquid soap and washing their hands with it. Therefore, you may need to monitor their hand-washing activities until they learn to wash their hands without using too much liquid soap and making a mess.

11 ✳ Get Everything You Can up off Floors and Counters

Having less to move in order to clean floor and counter surfaces will dramatically decrease routine clean-up time. Here are some ways to get things up and off floors and counters to make cleaning easier:

- Make use of under-the-cupboard kitchen appliance models instead of those that sit on the counter surface such as coffeemakers, can openers, microwaves, hand-held mixers, etc.

- Make use of walls to keep things up off the floor. Install wall lamps instead of floor lamps. Hang brooms, mops, rakes, and tools on the wall. Anything that has a handle can have a hole drilled in it and be kept on the wall by a nail.

- Install shelving and Peg-Boards in children's rooms to keep toys and games up off the floor.

- Use built-ins whenever possible: bathroom scales, ironing units, toasters, towel holders and storage compartments are all available as built-in units. If your home is being built or remodeled, consider how much you can have built into the walls so you don't have to clean around and under things.

- Have larger appliances (range, refrigerator, trash compactor, dishwasher, microwave) built in. This gives you the added advantage of only having the front surface to clean rather than having to clean the sides and areas between appliances.

- Hang a pail under the sink to hold useful items such as cleaning supplies, a first aid kit, and spare toilet tissue.

- Hang hooks and racks on the backs of doors: pajamas, robes, and jackets can easily be kept up off the floor and out of sight this way. Be sure hooks are within reach of the person using the room.

- Put racks inside the doors under sinks to hold rags.

- Hang up items of awkward shapes and sizes (like vacuum attachments, blow dryers, curling irons, sports equipment for another season, and so on) in nylon mesh bags, heavy-duty plastic trash bags, or duffel bags.

- Hang wire racks or mesh bags around the shower head to hold shampoo, a razor, a pumice stone, and other bath accessories.

- Hang bicycles on bicycle hooks whenever they are not in use. You can buy these hooks at most hardware stores and bicycle shops. They are easy to install, and they are easy to use for family members who can lift the weight of their bicycles. Hanging bicycles on the wall of the garage gives you more space and makes it much easier to sweep the floor.

- Store unused or seldom-used items such as family memorabilia up high and out of sight instead of in boxes at eye level in the garage or in storage spaces. An attic is great for this kind of storage. If your house doesn't have an attic, you can create shelving by placing heavy-duty plywood over the rafters in the garage. Use this space for out-of-the-way, long-term storage.

12 ＊ Simplify the Way You Clean House

- Allow timesaving devices and products to save you time and energy.

- Use microwave and cooking systems that allow you to prep, cook, serve, store, and freeze in the same dishwasher-safe containers. Tupperware's stack cooker is designed to cook a three-course meal in twenty-five minutes. The cookware then goes from microwave to table to refrigerator to dishwasher for easy clean-up.

- Water-softening equipment makes all cleaning jobs easier and can cut cleaning time in half.

- Decide if there is work that can be reduced or eliminated entirely. Instead of spraying every piece of furniture when dusting, spray the dust rag and make a quick job of it.

- Your rubber bath and sink mats can be washed in the washing machine with your towels rather than having to be scrubbed by hand. Some shower curtains may also wash and dry well in your machine, as long as you put a few towels in with them.

- Think about everything you do before you do it and ask yourself if there might be an easier way.

- Try doing things less often and see if there is a noticeable effect. If you usually vacuum daily, see if you could get by with vacuuming twice weekly. If you are in the habit of ironing your sheets, consider only ironing the top third of the sheet.

- Check to see how you can update your familiar routine using the time- and energy-saving products on the market today.

13 * Write Out a Housekeeping Schedule

Writing out a detailed housekeeping schedule has many benefits for any type of housekeeper. You are never completely finished because people live in your home and your home is in a universe in which (as one of the laws of thermodynamics explains) everything is constantly going from a state of order to a state of chaos. Housekeeping is the attempt to keep chaos at bay so your family can enjoy some order. For the perfectionist, a housekeeping schedule draws the line, telling you when you have done enough for today. For the person who has grown to accept living amidst the chaos, it defines where to start and what needs to be done to create order.

Writing out a schedule is a way of formalizing your goals. You become specific, envision the completion of each task, give yourself a time frame, and are able to measure results. If you have never used a written schedule it may take a few weeks before you discipline yourself to respond to the schedule, but don't give up. Just having the written schedule, even if you don't accomplish it all, will help you begin mentally to picture what you need to do to keep your house looking great. Once you have the picture clearly in mind it will be easier to make it a reality. You can customize a schedule for your family:

1. Look at each room or area in your home (include the garage, basement, attic, patio, tool shed, stor-

age shed, whatever is part of your responsibility) and list everything that needs to be done to keep it looking great. (If you don't know, refer to a book on home maintenance that has a standard list from which to work.)

2. Decide how often those things need to be done (according to the needs of your family): daily, weekly, seasonally, or annually.

3. Decide who will be responsible for doing those tasks. This can include hired help. Just schedule their visits into your overall housekeeping schedule.

4. On a weekly basis, look over your general schedule and assign specific tasks to each day of the week. (Be sure to give your family one day to rest without any obligations.) Write out the schedule and post it prominently.

5. Do what you are scheduled to do when you are scheduled to do it, and make sure everyone else does what they are supposed to do when they are supposed to do it.

Remember to allow some flexibility until you find a schedule that works for your family. Allow family members to have some say in terms of when they do their part and what they want to do (within reason). Make some provision for trading jobs when necessary.

14 ∗ Stop Dirt and Clutter at the Source

The more dirt and clutter you keep out, the less you will have to clean up. Here are some strategies to stop dirt and clutter at the source:

- Studies show the single best way to cut cleaning time is to have every entrance to your home covered by vinyl- or rubber-backed doormats, inside and out. Make sure the mats are sturdy. Commercial grade mats are best. Cover the entire area leading to each door, or step approaching a door, including garage entrances. Vacuum or shake mats daily.

- Have children (running in and out all day) leave their shoes outside the door.

- Shut windows.

- During bad weather, use alternate entryways or "mudrooms" to collect dirt before it gets inside your home.

- Use your oven vent to suck grease and grime away before it has a chance to settle in your kitchen.

- Use your air conditioner. It helps filter out dust and dirt. Be sure to change or clean the filters often (check every two to three months) or regularly vacuum the filters with the dust brush attachment on your vacuum. If you have central air and heat, arrange to have the system checked and maintained by a service technician. Consult your dealer for a suggested maintenance schedule.

- Toss all junk mail before it enters the house. Keep a trash can somewhere between your mailbox and your front door. Decide what constitutes junk mail and make a commitment not to bring it into your home.

- Use an errand drawer to house small items that are left around while waiting for something to be done with them: the barrettes left by the girl next door, coupons for shopping, photographs you don't want to forget to take next time you visit your mother.

15 * Keep Messes to a Minimum

Messes will be made in every home. You can hardly do anything without making some sort of mess. If you try never to have messes in your home you will eliminate some of the most pleasurable experiences of life, such as baking, cooking, crafts, artwork, building a model airplane, and finger-painting.

Though you don't want to live mess-free, you can aim to contain the messes so that you have less to clean after an enjoyable bout of mess-making. Here are some tips and ideas:

- Keep all potential mess-making materials out of reach of children. Just as you would kid-proof your home for the safety and protection of your children, kid-proof your home from the messes children make. This includes keeping markers, paints, crayons, and glue put up where children can't reach them, having specific areas where children are allowed to eat, not having gum accessible to small children, and keeping cosmetics out of reach.

- Limit entertaining guests or children at play to specified rooms or parts of the house. In this way you can quickly pick up the limited area, or you can close it off until later and the rest of your house still looks great.

- Buy only washable crayons, washable markers, water-based paints, and other art supplies that are easy to clean.

- Use coasters, trivets, doilies, trays, and napkins to protect wood surfaces so that you don't have to work at removing rings or refinishing marred wood surfaces.

- Place pet dishes on vinyl or rubber mats so the mess is contained.

- If you have a messy job to do inside the house be sure to cover floors with tarp or newspaper. The time you invest in keeping the mess off the floor will usually be less than the time it would take to clean the mess up.

- Keep a vinyl tablecloth around to use as a boundary marker for children playing with molding clay. The crumbs of molding clay that harden can be picked up in the tablecloth (instead of being ground into your carpet) and thrown away. Then just wipe the cloth and put it away. This tablecloth also works well instead of newspaper under any art project.

- Fold children's play clothes and pajamas together in sets so that they don't have the opportunity to mess up several drawers when getting ready for bed or play.

- Require children to eat at places designed for them, such as a high chair, a small table, or a bar where they are able to reach their food easily. Also use dishes and utensils that help prevent messes children typically make while eating. For example, use cups and tumblers (named that for a reason) with sipper lids, which make it almost impossible to spill a drink even if it is knocked over.

16 ✳ Simplify Your Decorating Style

With a busy schedule, it's worth the effort to develop an appreciation for smooth clean lines and spacious views. Even if you have lived with a particular style of decorating for many years you can develop a taste for styles that are easier to keep clean. Here are some ideas:

- If your decorating style includes small trinkets or other knickknacks that require constant dusting, enclose them in a curio cabinet where you can enjoy their beauty but not spend as much time dusting.

- Choose furniture and decorating items with an eye for how easy they are to maintain and clean.

- Use stain-resistant fabrics on all furniture.

- Use carpet treated with stain repellent or apply stain repellent yourself.

- Choose medium color, low-pile carpets. These show less dirt and are easier to maintain.

- Use smooth surfaces over rough ones whenever possible. They collect less dirt and are easier to keep clean.

- Use washable wall coverings, high-gloss paint, and washable wallpaper.

- Consider using shades rather than blinds on some windows, as shades are easier to clean.

- For fresh ideas on decorating your home in easy-to-clean fashion, tour model homes. Often the decorating schemes in model homes feature clean lines and spacious views. You may be inspired to change your decorating style once you have some specific decorating ideas in mind to substitute for that which is familiar in your home.

17 ✳ Have Family Members Clean Up After Themselves

One of the best ways to keep your house looking great is to have members of your household accept personal responsibility for cleaning up after themselves as much as possible. This helps everyone develop good habits, reduces the potential for conflict (as in, "That's not MY mess! Susie used the bathroom last. Why should I have to pick up after her?"), and makes housekeeping manageable. Obviously, there will be occasions when this rule is not followed to perfection, but if you set this as the norm for your family, you will be miles ahead.

Here are some basic routines that can be taught and expected:

- *Bath time.* Part of taking a bath or shower is wiping down the tub or shower walls before you get out. Have children collect bath toys and place them in a mesh bag that can be hung up on the shower head.

- *Clothing.* Clothes are to be put in a hamper if dirty or put away if clean.

   After laundry is folded, it can be placed in plastic crates or bins in the laundry area that are labeled for each person. When taking clothes out of the dryer, fold and put items in the assigned bin; then family members can become responsible for taking their clean clothing into their rooms and putting it away themselves.

Train them to straighten drawers every time they put something away. This is easier if you use drawer dividers to indicate where various types of clothes belong (socks, underwear, shirts, shorts, pajamas, and so on).

- *Meals and snacks.* Take dishes to the sink, scrape, rinse, and put them in the dishwasher, or stack them to be washed later. Throw away all paper or trash from snacks. Put away unfinished items properly.

- *Bedding.* Make the bed each morning. You can make this task easy for small children by using comforters rather than bedspreads, which easily show wrinkles.

18 ✳ Make Home Maintenance As Easy As Possible

The easier it is to do the job of maintaining your home, the easier it will be to get everyone to do her part. Try to make it easier to do it right than it is to do it wrong. Here are some suggestions:

- Have wastebaskets in every room and specified use area in your home. If there is a study area in a larger room, have a wastebasket near the desk and at another spot in the room where other activities take place.

- Have hampers in every bedroom and bathroom. Require them to be used regularly.

- Make things easier to put away than they are to get out. For example, give children plastic bins on the floor of their closet to keep their shoes in. When children can toss shoes where they belong instead of having to place them up somewhere or carefully put them on a shoe tree, the job will easily become a good habit. Put like objects in storage crates or bins (puzzles, blocks, dolls, and so on).

- Have a long-handled sponge for everyone to use to wipe out the tub without having to get down on hands and knees.

- Provide a step stool for children to be able to reach the sink so they can rinse and stack dishes after snacks and meals.

- Keep a small shower head on a rubber hose attached to the spigot in each tub. This helps children rinse their hair after a shampoo and also makes rinsing the tub easier after it has been cleaned. This can also cut down on bath time if you want to make a quick job of the bath rather than always combining bath and play time.

- Provide a net bag to collect all bath toys after the bath. Even young children can learn to put their toys in the bag at the end of a bath. This will not only save time, it may save your back!

- If coats and galoshes are routinely thrown down on a table in the entryway, move the table. In its place arrange several coatracks within easy reach of everyone and plastic-lined baskets to collect apparel.

- Keep children's shelves, drawers, clothes rods, and so on at a level they can reach.

- Keep a laundry hamper (inside) or large plastic trash can (outside) so children can throw toys in the container after playing with them. Then at the end of play time or before their bedtime story, help them put away the toys where they belong.

- Store dishes as near as possible to the dishwasher or dish draining rack.

- Organize your kitchen on the basis of point of need, placing items as close as possible to where they will be used.

19 * A Stitch in Time Saves Nine

Any job that is left undone over the course of time becomes more difficult, either in actuality or psychologically (as you wrestle with procrastination). Making a habit of dealing with problems and needs within your home as soon as you notice them will save you a great deal of time in the long run. Here are some specific ways to put the old adage "A stitch in time saves nine" into practice:

- Clean up messes as soon as they occur. Don't wait until the spilled orange juice has attracted ants or the stain has had time to set. If an accident happens, stop whatever you are doing and attend to cleaning it up immediately.

- Don't allow the passage of time to make more work for you. Food allowed to dry on dishes is harder to remove. You can create a habit of rinsing dishes immediately as easily as adopting the habit of putting dishes in the sink without being rinsed. Whenever you put dishes in the dishwasher but need to wait to have a full load before washing them, push the rinse-and-hold button.

- When something is broken, fix it immediately. A wobbly shelf left unattended can easily become a counter and floor full of shattered glassware. A dripping pipe can turn into a minor flood and ruined carpeting. If you put off fixing something because you don't know how, call someone who does know how to help or hire someone. You will still be ahead in time and money saved by paying now rather than paying later.

- Practice routine maintenance. Read the manuals on all household appliances and schedule maintenance into your home management plans.

- Learn to do things right the first time around, so you don't have to do them over. For example, when loading the dishwasher, the right way is to place large bowls and plastics on the top rack so the water can reach the dishes on the top and so the intense heat doesn't melt the plastics. If you put large bowls on the bottom, you will have to rewash the dishes above them. If you put plastics on the bottom, they may melt.

20 * Educate Yourself and Your Family

Just as you must develop skills to accomplish any worthwhile endeavor, learning how to keep your home looking nice in the midst of a hectic lifestyle requires education. This may mean learning skills that are entirely new or adapting skills to fit your busy schedule. This also includes educating your family in the basics of home maintenance. Here are some ideas for including continuing education in your family home maintenance plan:

- Define and post expectations for home maintenance that everyone will be taught to follow. Have a cleaning checklist in each room (posted in an out-of-the-way spot, such as inside a cabinet or behind a door). As children become old enough to take on cleaning jobs, teach them how to do each task on the checklist in the proper way.

- Follow the four-step teaching progression: (1) I do it and you watch, (2) I do it and you help me, (3) you do it and I help you, (4) you do it and I do something else.

- Use these resources to educate yourself and your family:

- Library books offer a wide selection of information to teach you how to do almost anything from dusting to decorating. Get each person in your family a library card and head for the housekeeping books.
- Magazines are full of household hints and helps. You can subscribe to a popular home or women's magazine, or you can browse through past issues at the library.
- Seminars are a fast, easy way to focus on household organization, time management, holiday preparation, and many other homemaking topics. Radio talk shows that deal with home and family issues are a good source of leads to find seminars of this sort, along with the home section of your local paper.
- College extension courses on home management are available. Some are for college credit, others are not. If you are not concerned with credits, you may be able to audit for-credit classes at a lower rate.
- Children's resources such as the book and video *The Berenstain Bears and the Messy Room* are available. Check with your local library or children's bookstore.
- Resource books kept on hand can help you whenever you have a question about a particular problem. A couple of good ones are *The Woman's Day Help Book: The Complete How-to for the Busy Housekeeper* and *Confessions of a Happily Organized Family*. Before buying a book to keep on hand, see if you can check it out from your library to consider whether it would be useful as a reference.

21 * Eliminate Work Before It Is Created

Spare yourself! There are times when you can make choices that eliminate your work before it is created. Find them and use them.

- Buy only wash-and-wear fabrics, linens, and table-cloths that machine wash and need little or no ironing.

- Take advantage of no-wax floors. You may never wax again!

- Always ask yourself: Is there a way to accomplish this goal or get the effect I want without doing as much work? If you want shining wood floors in your entryway there are two ways you can get them. You can choose a polished wood and regularly wax the floor, or you can get a wood floor with a polyurethane finish. The second option requires dusting and an occasional wiping with a cleaning solution. You get the same impressive effect and spare yourself hours of hard work.

- Familiarize yourself with time-saving products. Grocery market shelves and advertisements are full of claims to save you time and energy. Browse the cleaning aisle of your market and try some of the products you've never used before.

- Buy appliances that do much of the work for you, such as self-cleaning ovens, self-defrosting refrigerators.

- Use toilet bowl sanitizer regularly.

- If your family is in the habit of throwing towels in the laundry every time they use them to dry off clean bodies after bathing, teach them to use their towels twice before laundering. Provide plenty of towel racks, and label towels by name if necessary (sometimes children are "cootie-conscious" and can't fathom using a towel that may have been touched by a brother or sister). Just make sure towels are hung up to dry promptly after use, and your laundry load will be reduced significantly.

22 ＊ Become a Dust-Buster

Dusting can be done quickly and easily by using a few simple tools. Gone are the days when you needed to take the rugs out and beat the dust out of them. Today you can suck the dust and dirt away rather than just moving it around. Here's how:

- Remove as much dust and dirt as possible by taking it out of the room permanently. Instead of sweeping and using a dust pan to collect the dust, change to using an electric broom, vacuum, and mini-vac.

- Never use a feather duster or dust cloth without using a dusting spray that traps the dust and allows you to pick it up. You can spray your feather duster, your dust cloth, or your furniture directly.

- Use a small mop to dust the high spots (even a children's toy mop will do). Be sure to spray the mop with dusting spray so that it will attract and catch the dust rather than just spread it around. Use this to reach tops of furniture, high picture frames, and other wall units out of reach.

- If dust tends to collect under your bed, try spreading a shower curtain under the bed (hidden away by the dust ruffle). Once each week, carefully remove the shower curtain, fold it, and carry the dust outside, or slide the curtain out and vacuum before returning it to catch the dust for another week.

• Take a quick dust-buster tour of your home. Arm yourself with a cleaning apron containing a mini-vac, dust cloth, feather duster, and small dust mop (all sprayed with dusting cleaner). Turn on the air conditioner to filter dust that becomes airborne. Start in one room and work from top to bottom either in a circle around the room or from one side of the room to another. Move quickly from room to room collecting dust and floating dirt wherever it is found. Use the mini-vac to remove dust from window sills, blinds, corners, and other hard-to-reach areas. Collect pet hair from furniture and drapes.

• Vacuum floors and doormats.

23 * Make Things Sparkle

When a house sparkles, it looks great. If you focus your attention on making things sparkle, no one may ever notice that you didn't have time for a thorough cleaning. We're talking shiny floors, flawless mirrors, polished picture frames, glittering glass, and sparkling faucets and knobs.

Get your apron ready with these supplies: glass cleaner, furniture polish on a cloth, all-purpose cleaner, paper towels, a hand-held squeegee. Enter each room with an eye for anything you can make sparkle. Then systematically move through the room doing all of the following:

- Buff all faucets using all-purpose cleaner and paper towels.

- Wash and dry sinks, polishing the drain.

- Clean all mirrors from top to bottom using glass cleaner and a squeegee. Be sure to dry the squeegee with a paper towel after each swipe from top down. Rub with a paper towel to clear up any lines left from the squeegee. Dry the bottom of the mirror so puddles of glass cleaner are picked up.

- Spot-clean floors with spray all-purpose cleaner and a paper towel or damp mop if you have time.

- Remove cobwebs from glass lighting fixtures and clean with glass cleaner and paper towels.

- Clean the glass on all doors.

- Polish picture frames and clean glass with glass cleaner so those shining faces really shine!

- Clean glass on televisions, computers, and entertainment units.

- Polish all other shiny surfaces (front of appliances, brass, and so on) until they sparkle.

24 ✳ Freshen Up

Fresh and clean go together. Whenever you freshen up your home in any way, it makes the whole environment seem nicer. Whether it's a fresh scent or fresh flowers, freshness is a sign of beauty. Here are some ideas for freshening up your home:

- Empty soap dishes and put out new soap. Use decorative guest soaps that are pleasing to the people using that bathroom most often.

- Put out fresh towels—and not just when company is coming.

- Put fresh flowers in every room. You can buy one mixed bouquet and turn it into several small ones throughout your home. A single rose can speak volumes. Or try a floating gardenia in a lovely shallow bowl filled with water to dramatically freshen up the scent of a room.

- Put out fresh potpourri in bowls or baskets throughout your house. You can buy new potpourri or freshen up the potpourri you already have by adding a few drops of scent available at craft supply stores.

- Put down freshly washed throw rugs throughout the house. You may want to have duplicate sets of rugs so you can wash one set while the fresh set is on duty.

- Fresh scents: Try simmering spices like cinnamon, cloves, and nutmeg on the stove for creating a warm, lovely atmosphere (even when you don't have time to bake).

- Occasionally use baking soda or carpet freshener to keep your carpets smelling fresh. Sprinkle the baking soda or carpet freshening powder on the carpet, wait fifteen minutes, and vacuum. Fresh-smelling carpets make your home seem cleaner.

- Use solid continuous air fresheners, particularly in bathrooms.

- Freshen kitchen smells by occasionally grinding up the peel of a lemon, lime, grapefruit, or orange in the garbage disposal. Rinse refrigerator walls (after washing) with rinse water and lemon extract.

- Eliminate odors at their source: remove tired flowers and dispose of the water, empty the litter box regularly, change the bird cage lining, empty the garbage frequently, spray shower curtains with disinfectant deodorizing spray, dispose of diapers in a pail outside immediately upon changing baby.

- When your spray perfume is almost gone and you can't squeeze another drop out of the bottle, remove the lid and set the bottle in the bottom of a laundry hamper. As the tiny bit of perfume evaporates, it will give a lovely fragrance to your laundry.

- Air out rooms daily except during bad weather. Each morning when you begin your daily routine, open curtains, drapes, blinds, shades, and windows to allow fresh air to circulate in your home.

25 ✳ Give Yourself a Realistic Schedule

To keep your house looking great you need a personal schedule for each day, even if you don't end up sticking to it exactly. Having a structured schedule will keep you moving when you need to and free you up to rest when you might otherwise push yourself to exhaustion.

- Your schedule should start with the basics: time for sleeping, eating, grooming, exercise, and rest. Write out approximate times for each of these in a typical week.

- Next, schedule in your ongoing commitments that occur on a regular basis: work, classes, church, and so on.

- Schedule time to nurture the important relationships in your life: time daily with each child, a heart-to-heart chat with your spouse, visiting extended family and friends. These are moments when you don't want to be concerned with doing something else at the same time.

- Schedule thirty minutes in the morning before you leave the house to straighten up your bedroom (ten minutes), clear breakfast dishes and tidy up the kitchen (ten minutes), give your bathroom a basic once-over (five minutes), and move quickly through the house straightening whatever is noticeably out of place and inspecting the efforts of other family members (five minutes). Granted, you will need to practice this routine to keep it under thirty minutes. However, once your family gets into the routine of leaving the house looking nice when they leave for the day, the reward of coming home to a clean house will continue to encourage you.

- Give yourself time after each meal to put things right in the kitchen.

- Give yourself and your family time before bed to pick up and put away whatever is out of place from that day.

- Schedule one specific chore from your weekly plan each day for each family member to keep your house looking great.

- Post your schedule in a prominent place and use stars or stickers to award completed work.

- Make your schedule realistic. You cannot expect to keep your house looking great without any time and effort. If you plan approximately one hour daily for adults and twenty to thirty minutes for children to help with home management you should be fine. If you do this consistently, you will occasionally need to set aside a larger block of time for special projects, but for the most part your house will stay nice and will continually be a comfortable place to live.

- Firmly schedule a day off each week when everyone is free to relax and not do any chores.

- Be sure to schedule some time just to relax and appreciate the order, beauty, and comfort your home maintenance schedule provides!

26 * Economize Your Time

Time is a valuable commodity. Learning to make the most of your time will help you keep your house looking great. Here are some ways to economize your time.

- Do more than one thing at a time when possible. Here are some examples:

    - If you have a portable phone, do small jobs that can be done quietly with one hand (carry out garbage, dust, buff faucets, arrange fresh flowers) while talking on the phone.
    - Fold laundry or do other stationary work while watching television.
    - Do you like the feel of freshly ironed bed sheets and pillow cases but don't have the time to iron them the way your mother used to? Try ironing your other clothes on top of a pillow case or sheet folded in quarters. Turn the sheet each time you iron a new item and by the time your regular ironing is finished your bedding will be too.
    - If you have a baby or small child who tends to wet his bedding regularly, buy a few extra crib mattress liners and sheets. When you make the bed for the night layer several sets of mattress

liners and sheets. When the bed is wet in the middle of the night you can simply remove the top sheet and liner without the extra work of replacing them.

- If you commute to work, consider taking the train or bus or carpooling. Not only will you be doing something to help the environment, you can use the time you are not driving to get some work done.

- If you tend to stay on the phone too long because you have a hard time telling someone you need to get off, set a timer for the amount of time you can afford for chatting. If you accept a call, set your timer and when it goes off simply explain that you have to go, your time is gone.

- Use an answering machine at home to screen your calls if you find phone calls sidetrack you when you are in the middle of some project. If you have a set time to return your calls you will save yourself time in two ways. First, you will not have to take time to get your attention focused back on whatever you were doing after being interrupted by a phone call. Second, when you give yourself a set amount of time to return all your calls, you are less likely to waste time making calls longer than they need to be.

- Keep a running inventory of items to buy when you go shopping or run errands. Invite family members to add to the list anything they need or use the last of. Always take this list with you when you go to the store or run errands. If you rely on your memory alone, you may forget something. Forgetting even one item can mean another trip to the grocery store at an inopportune moment.

27 * Take Control of Clutter

Clean out: Aim to de-clutter one closet, drawer, cupboard or room. Here's how:

1. Call your local thrift store, Salvation Army, or charity that will pick up discarded items. Schedule a pick-up for tomorrow.

2. Give yourself four containers for trash, things to put away in another room (later), things to sell or give away, and things you aren't sure whether you want to keep or not.

3. Remind yourself of the function each area serves. Consider who will use it, what will be done there, and what should not be done there. For example, the children's chest of drawers should keep current clothing available so they can dress easily and without crisis each morning. This definition of function dictates that hair accessories, dolls, birds' nests, and other items should go elsewhere.

4. Ask yourself if an item is used regularly. If it is not used regularly, it goes in the sell/give away, not sure, or trash container. Don't give in to the temptation of dealing with the items you are not sure about or putting away items that go elsewhere. Just

keep your focus on making this one area conform to the function you envision for it. Make this one area look great before you tackle your other containers.

5. If possible, immediately get rid of the give-away items so you aren't faced with carting them around or reconsidering your decision. Immediately throw away the trash.

6. Put the "not sure" container out of reach for two weeks. If you can, give it away without opening it. If not, take some time to go through it with the goal of giving away half of what you've collected. Then try to store the rest without bringing it back into your house.

Here are some more un-cluttering tips:

•   Decide how important your clutter is to you, compared to the amount of time, money, stress, and effort required to store all your stuff or to clean around it.

•   Start every cleaning task by removing all clutter.

•   Make clutter reducing choices: Read the newspaper at the office or library instead of letting papers accumulate around the house. Also, don't have tables and countertops at entryways. They become a tempting place to toss whatever may be coming through the door.

•   Have clutter reduction competition. Have a family competition every three months to see how much unnecessary stuff each one can eliminate from the household. Give prizes for the one who eliminates the most, the one most improved, the most clutter-free room, and good clutter-reducing ideas.

- Have a place for paperwork and bills that is contained and out of sight (bill boxes, letter trays, inside a rolltop desk, transferred to computer, and so on).

- Consider confiscating anything left out of place on a daily basis with fines to be paid by anyone wishing to retrieve items or with rewards to anyone without any clutter collected.

28 ✳ Fifteen-Minute Kitchen Clean-Up After Meals

The key to keeping your house looking great is to practice undoing the daily damage caused by actually living in and enjoying your home. Your family can easily be taught to get the kitchen back in top condition after every meal if you practice a simple routine such as the one below. Although they may complain at first if this is new for them, you can use these daily times together to build relationships, listen to your children, and even have some fun. Here's a basic routine you can adapt to your own preferences:

1. Clear and wipe the table (having all family members routinely bus their own dishes if they are old enough).

2. Scrape and rinse dishes. Stack dishes in preparation for washing in the sink, or load dishwasher and set on rinse and hold.

3. Fill pots with water and leave to soak (don't waste time scrubbing until the food is softened and loosened up for you). You'll be ahead of the game if you get in the habit of allowing pots and pans to soak while you eat.

4. Put all leftover food away where it belongs.

5. Spray the range top, microwave, appliances, and counters with spray cleaner. Wipe surfaces clean. Wipe out the inside of the microwave oven with warm water after each use.

6. Sprinkle cleanser on any stubborn spots or stains.

7. Carry out garbage (be sure to keep extra liners in the bottom of the pail for immediate access), and replace the plastic trash liner.

8. Wipe away cleanser and rinse pots and pans (if they are ready).

9. Sweep, vacuum, or damp mop the kitchen floor.

Here are some additional items you might choose to add to the basic clean-up plan:

• Reset the table for the next meal. Even small children can help with this by arranging place mats and napkins, items that they cannot break. This gives you the added advantage of making your table attractive at all times.

• Clean windows over the sink with glass cleaner if necessary.

29 ✳ Ten Minutes to Bedroom Beauty

For most people, the bedroom is a place to retreat from the world, rejuvenate, spend intimate time with their spouses, refresh themselves, and prepare to face the world looking their best each day. Because of all these uses, it's important to keep your bedroom in order so that you can be comfortable there. With a few simple habits, you can keep your bedroom looking beautiful in only ten minutes each morning.

Here are a few tips that will help keep major messes from accumulating in the bedroom:

- Decorate each bedroom in a way that is pleasing to the person who lives in it. Take each person's preferences seriously when decorating. If the occupant has a personal connection to how the room looks when it is at its best, he will be more easily induced to keep it looking tip-top.

- Have a hamper in each bedroom (as well as in bathrooms that are used heavily), and require everyone to use the hamper immediately when clothes are removed. Be vigilant about not tolerating clothes being thrown on the floor. If you train children this way while they are young, you may have less of a fight on your hands when they become teenagers.

- Have a wastebasket in every bedroom. Be sure to line it with plastic liners and keep extras in the bottom of the trash container. This makes it easy to keep it clean each day.

- If someone likes to read or write in the room, have a place for books, magazines, papers, stationery, and other items close at hand. Provide attractive magazine racks, bookcases (near where reading is done), and a contained stationery caddie to prevent piles of paper and books from getting out of hand.

- Use comforters or quilts instead of bedspreads, especially for children. It is much easier to make a bed look nice when you don't have to worry about every wrinkle showing. When it is easier to get the desired results, it will be easier to create a habit of never leaving the house with a bed unmade.

These mess-preventing measures should keep the bedroom manageable. This ten-minute morning routine should do the rest:

1. Straighten the bed and fluff pillows.

2. Pick up and put away clothing (items fresh from the laundry or any clothing that missed the hamper).

3. Carry a bag with you and move in a circle around the room, collecting all trash and putting away books, magazines, jewelry, cosmetics, and other stray items.

4. Vacuum or use a mini-vac if necessary.

5. Use a dust cloth treated with dusting spray to dust furniture lightly. Remove dust from windowsills and blinds by using a treated feather duster or small dust mop.

30 * Ten Minutes to a Lovely Living Room

Your living room or family room is a place that is typically heavily used. Your family needs to feel comfortable enough to relax and have fun somewhere in your home. The living room or family room is usually the place for home entertainment, playing, watching television, and visiting with friends. Though you want your home comfortably clean, there will be times your family room or living room looks—well—lived in. However, using a few simple rules and a basic daily clean-up routine can keep that "lived in" look from becoming a mess.

Here are some basic rules you may want to consider for your home. Each family can adapt these to their specific needs and preferences. The point is that it helps to have guidelines for how to behave and care for these shared family areas.

- Don't eat in the living room unless you are using a TV tray or are seated on a vinyl table cloth (spread on the floor for children to use on special occasions).

- Put away whatever you bring into the living/family room before going on to do something else.

- Don't throw things or play in ways that might disturb the room.

- Use furniture only as it was intended.

You get the idea. Whatever rules you institute for your family, make sure they are reasonable, clearly understood, and consistently enforced.

Once you have a plan for keeping your living/family room livable, it should be easy to keep it clean. Use this ten-minute routine to keep your living room looking great:

1. Pick up everything that doesn't belong on the floor before you do anything else. Once the floor is clean the entire room appears more manageable, and you will be encouraged to continue.

2. Carry a bag with you to collect all trash as you quickly move around the room.

3. Pick up, put away, and straighten any items that belong in the living/family room but are out of place.

4. Collect all clutter belonging in other rooms into a container (a sturdy painted basket can even be worked into your living room decor and used daily for this purpose). At the end of each day, this basket can be carried from room to room until all out-of-place objects are back where they belong.

5. Dust as necessary.

6. Vacuum or use a mini-vac for spot-cleaning.

7. Use glass cleaner and paper towels to remove smudges and fingerprints from glass doors, mirrors, and glass furniture (such as the tops of coffee tables and the fronts of entertainment units).

31 * Use Emotional Energy When You Have It

There are times when you will experience a burst of energy that was unexpected. You may wake up feeling particularly refreshed, come home from the health club and find yourself bursting with energy from having exercised, or you may have a burst of energy for some unknown reason. Whenever you are feeling great, put that energy to use making your home look great. Just ask any expectant mother who is struck with the nesting instinct and feels driven to wash walls. By all means, don't ask questions. Strike while the iron is hot!

You may also have energy to burn when you are highly emotional. Some people naturally gravitate toward working out their anger by attacking a dirty house or a disorganized closet. Scrubbing hard, beating a rug, polishing wood until it gleams, throwing away trash, or sweeping the walkway can be a healthy outlet for the pent-up energy generated by anger. If you are not someone who does this naturally, try it. It sure beats destructive displays of anger that you will only have to clean up later.

Some people can use cleaning a room or making the house look nice as a way to lift them out of mild depression. If you are feeling down and as if your life is out of control, try taking control of one small area of your house. Start slow and tell yourself you are just going to make one small place nice for you. You may find that bringing order and beauty to your surroundings lifts your spirits. You may find that the act of getting up and moving can be a start to getting back to being your old self. (This is not to suggest that cleaning is a solution to chronic depression. There are times when people can't just pull themselves out of the doldrums and need medical help.)

Clean when you are happy or inspired. There are moments when you feel great and are inspired to demonstrate how great you feel with productive activities. If you have just been promoted or have read a magazine article that has inspired you to make your house look great, don't let the moment pass. Get up and go for it!

32 ∗ Plan Systems to Keep Your Home in Order

Webster's dictionary defines a system as "a group of objects or units so combined as to form a whole and work, or move interdependently and harmoniously." Within your home there is the need for systems to deal with the ongoing needs of your family. For these systems to serve you well they must accomplish an ongoing task, work interdependently and harmoniously. If your systems break down, disorder will be a regular part of your home life. Therefore, it is important to do a check-up on the basic ongoing systems for your home. Check to see if you have recurrent problems with any of these systems and do enough study and restructuring of your routines to fix the problem in the system. This saves you the time needed to continually deal with recurrent disorder. You will note that all systems are cyclical and ongoing.

Here are the basic systems necessary to make your home run smoothly:

- *Laundry:* Wash clothes—dry clothes—store clothes —wear clothes—collect dirty clothes—wash clothes . . .

- *Meals:* Plan meals—shop for food—prepare food— serve food—eat food—discard or save food—clean up—plan meals . . .

- *Garbage and dirt:* Live in our world—accumulate garbage and dirt—discard garbage and dirt (and recycle)—live in our world . . .

- *Home maintenance and repairs:* Live in your home —use your home—time takes its toll—things run down or break—maintain or repair your home—live in your home . . .

- *Dishes:* Get hungry—eat on dishes—rinse off food —wash dishes—dry dishes—store dishes—get hungry . . .

- *General pick-up:* Need or want to do something— get things out—use things—put things down—pick things up—put things away—need or want to do something . . .

- *Mail:* Need to communicate with others—send outgoing mail—receive incoming mail—get responses from outgoing mail—need to respond to incoming mail—decide what to do with barrage of incoming mail—need to communicate with others . . .

- *Family maintenance and repairs:* You need to establish systems to maintain and repair your home. Likewise, you need to establish systems to maintain communication, repair hurt feelings, and provide mutual support within your family. Plan a system that gives time and attention to solving personal problems, applauding accomplishments, giving recognition for personal growth and achievement, resolving interpersonal conflict between family members, and sharing your lives. This used to be done around the dinner table when the whole family was together. In today's fast-paced society, many families aren't able to be together for dinner every evening. Still, you need to find some way to facilitate maintaining the health of the people in your home as well as the home itself.

• If you have small children you would add a system to dispose of diapers and to keep toys accessible yet easily picked up and put away.

33 ✳ Teach Everyone the Right Way to Do Laundry

Everyone in your family wears clothes and should learn to care for them properly, even if someone else in the family takes on the major responsibility for doing the family laundry. If everyone helps by working within the laundry system you establish, whoever does the laundry will have an easier time of it. Here are the basics to doing laundry properly:

1. Sort laundry in four categories: whites (including prints on white backgrounds), pastels (including prints on pastel backgrounds), medium and bright colors, and dark colors. You may want to keep four laundry baskets or hampers available near the washer so people can sort laundry into the appropriate categories when they take their hampers to the laundry area.

2. Separate items with special needs: lint magnets, stained or heavily soiled items, hand washables. Pretreat stains with stain stick or spray, presoak as necessary. Wash heavily soiled items in a separate load so as not to dirty unsoiled clothes.

3. Wash on the proper setting with appropriate water temperature. If you sort as you collect laundry, any-

one you have trained can do a load of wash as soon as one of the baskets is filled.

4. Dry clothes in the dryer without overloading the machine. When you overload, it takes longer and produces more wrinkles, which means more work for you in the long run. If you want to minimize drying time, dry medium-sized loads consecutively so that the dryer remains warm.

5. Empty the dryer immediately:
   - Remove clothes to be ironed while slightly damp.
   - Hang up permanent-press clothes upon removal from dryer. Invest in a rack that attaches to your dryer to hold extra hangers and clothes being hung up directly from the dryer.
   - Fold other clothes as they come out of the dryer. Resolve never to take unfolded clothes away from the laundry area.
   - Use a stain stick to treat stains that need to wait until laundry day.

Here are a few basic rules to keep everyone on track when it comes to making your laundry system work smoothly:

- When getting undressed, put dirty clothes in the nearest hamper.

- When clothes you've worn can be worn again, put them where they belong.

- If your family keeps sorted baskets in the laundry room, don't put clothes in the wrong basket.

- Whenever you put away clothes, organize or straighten the drawer or closet you are putting them into.

34 * Plan Organized Storage for Easy Access

When you store things in an organized way you save yourself time coming and going. When things are stored in an orderly way, they are easier to find. People will be more willing to put things away if they are confident of where they belong and if storage is easily accessible. You also make your house look better by having things out of sight rather than sitting around the house until someone can figure out where they belong.

Here are some ideas for organizing storage in your home:

- Consider customizing your closets to get the easiest use of the space. You need to create a place for everything and keep everything in its place. You can hire someone to organize your closet and build customized closet space, or you can purchase organizers you install yourself. You can also buy hanging organizers to keep shoes, sweaters, ties, and other specific items neatly arranged.

- Spend some time browsing in your hardware or department store closet section to get some new ideas for easily accessible storage, shelving, and handy wall organizers.

- Keep things used together stored together: hammer and nails, broom and dustpan, mop and pails, envelopes and stamps.

- Keep items at point of use: extra toilet tissue in the bathroom, fresh underwear folded neatly in the bathroom so it's handy after the bath when you need it, robes hanging in the bathroom, extra bedding in the bedroom (under the bed if possible).

- Use drawer dividers, bins, and organizers to indicate where things belong by category. Toys can be divided into dolls, cars, action figures, puzzles, animals, building blocks, and so on. You can keep one tub or divider for automotive tools, another for household tools, another for plumbing supplies. A plastic tub with a lid can become a craft canister, holding an assortment of items needed for crafts, including aprons and clean-up supplies.

- Label or color-code items in a way that makes it easy for people to identify what they need or to whom something belongs.

- Use out-of-the-way spaces for planned storage. There are many convenient storage containers designed to fit under beds. A child's schoolwork from each year fits nicely into a large (say 26″ × 30″ or larger) artist's folder, which can slide behind their chest of drawers. As schoolwork and treasures come in throughout the year, toss them into the open envelope. At the end of the year, sort through and keep the best representation of that year's work, label it and hang it on a peg or rack in the garage.

Here are some general guidelines about what to store where:

- In the space from your thigh to your shoulders, keep things you use most often, things you must reach quickly, and items of medium weight.

- In the space from your shoulders up, keep things you don't use on a regular basis (like extra bedding or your large turkey platter) and lightweight items.

- In the space from your thighs down, keep heavy items and little-used items. Whenever lifting, be sure to bend your knees instead of lifting the weight with your back muscles, or you may spend some of your valuable time convalescing.

35 ❋ Store Things Properly

Not only is it important to have your storage space well organized, it helps to make sure things are stored properly. Storing things improperly can result in more work for you later, usually at a time when you are in need and don't have time to spare.

Here are some guidelines on the proper way to store things:

- Don't cram clothes into drawers or linens into cramped storage spaces. This will create wrinkles. It also makes for extra work when you pull out one item and have to pick up all the other items that fall out.

- Store knits folded neatly so they will keep their shape. If you want to hang them, be sure to use padded hangers rather than wire hangers.

- Store ties on a tie rack or a length of curtain rod attached to a closet wall or door. For extra protection for delicate ties, cover the rod with felt.

- When storing clothes and bedding at the end of a season, use dust bags, not plastic bags. Be sure to leave one end of the bag open so fabrics can breathe. Sealing bags tightly can produce mildew in some climates.

- Be sure fabrics and clothing are clean before being stored. Food or unwashed stains may attract insects.

- Special occasion linens (used once a year or less) should be washed and rinsed thoroughly before storing but not ironed and starched. Ironed folds, when left for long periods of time, break down the fibers and, if the fabric has not been rinsed thoroughly, the soap residue tends to accumulate odors and cause yellowing. Putting a half cup of vinegar in the final rinse helps rid the material of leftover soap or detergent. When that special occasion arrives, your time invested in storing these precious items properly will pay off in time you will not spend restoring them to their original beauty.

- When hanging up bedspreads or pressed tablecloths, cut the cardboard tube from wrapping paper, paper towels, or wax paper lengthwise on one side. Slip this over a hanger and place the item to be stored over the tube. This will keep a crease from forming in the fabric.

- Customize your kitchen cabinets for the orderly storage of foodstuffs. Use canisters for staples such as flour, sugar, rice, pasta, and so on. Tupperware and Rubbermaid have full lines of plastic storage containers that preserve food and keep it within reach in an orderly fashion. Tupperware representatives offer to help customize kitchen storage without charge when you purchase their products. Other professionals are available for a fee to help you get kitchen storage in order.

36 ✻ Allow Chemicals to Do the Work for You

The supermarket cleaning aisles are full of cleaning supplies for particular uses. The chemists employed by these companies work long and hard finding chemicals to help you clean almost any household problem area. However, their research does you no good if you don't take the time to familiarize yourself with which products are best for dealing with a particular problem.

- Whenever a stain or cleaning problem occurs, identify what caused the problem. You can't choose the right solution if you don't know what caused the problem you want to remedy.

- Teach small children never to hide a spill or stain. If you get to the problem immediately, you have a much better chance of choosing the proper chemical and of giving that chemical the best chance of working.

- Get a basic housekeeping guide that includes a section on what kinds of chemicals work best on which types of cleaning problems.

- Give chemicals time to work. Seventy-five percent of all soil removal is done by using the proper cleaning solutions or chemicals and allowing them time to work. Don't waste time scrubbing. Instead of scrubbing immediately after spraying a surface, spray the surface and allow the solution to do its work for a few moments while you do something else. When you return, you will most likely only need to wipe the surface as opposed to scrubbing.

- Be sure to follow label directions and use the proper ratio of cleaning solution to water for those solutions you mix yourself. Keep all cleaning supplies out of reach of children.

- To clean mini-blinds or venetian blinds with a minimum of time and effort (every six months or so): Remove blinds from the window and place them in the bathtub with detergent or cleaning solution. Allow them to soak for twenty minutes. Then take them outside and hose them thoroughly. Hang them on a clothesline or from a ladder to air dry before rehanging.

37 * Lighten Up and Brighten Up

Lighting and bright colors can go a long way to enhance the appearance of your home. You can learn to make the most of natural lighting, indoor lighting of various sorts, and bright colors to bring a dull room to life. Here are some ideas on ways you can lighten up and brighten up your home:

- Popular decorating, home, and women's magazines usually have features on lightening up and brightening up your home decor during the spring months. Go to your local library periodicals section and browse through several spring issues for ideas you can use any time of year.

- Be creative with the use of light inside your home. Consider the diverse effects you can get with lighting. Visit a lamp and lighting store or department with an eye for lighting that would fit in with your decorating style. Look for ways you can substitute low maintenance lighting for other forms that require more time-consuming care (such as crystal chandeliers). Consider where you could use overhead lighting, track lighting, and wall lighting in place of floor lamps or table lamps. Lighting that is up off the floor saves you the time and trouble of cleaning around it.

- Use light, bright colors to enhance the look of your home. Paint the trim of your house and highlight your porch and yard or garden area with white paint (white planters, white screen, white scalloped brick around the flower beds, fresh white paint on the shutters).

- Let in as much natural light as possible, use skylights, draw your drapes back to allow the sunshine in.

- Use stenciling or sponge paints to add simple beauty to any room where you want to brighten things up without incurring a major expense.

- Allow as much light as possible into your home when cleaning. In this way you will be sure to see all the dirt and dust that needs to be dealt with. Even if you don't get it all, every time you clean, you will be able to use the light to help you see what you need to clean.

- Use candles and related pieces to give your home that special glow that only candlelight can give. Use votive candles in the bathroom, elegant centerpieces on the dining table, romantic candlelight in the bedroom, candlesticks on the mantle, and so on. When using candles, always be aware of the fire hazard and never leave children unattended in a room where candles are burning.

- Use brightly-colored throw pillows to liven up a dull room. If possible, tie the color to other accent pieces such as a colorful framed print.

38 ✳ Reconsider Priorities and Goals

Priorities are those things you value, placed in order of importance. Goals are specific dreams you are willing to take action on and plan to accomplish within a set time frame. Here are some things to think about regarding your priorities and goals in relation to keeping your house looking great:

- You make choices in life about how to use your resources of time, energy, and money. Typically whenever you cut back on what you are willing to spend in one area, you need to spend more in another area to compensate. If saving money is a high priority for you, you will probably have to spend more time and energy to keep your house looking great. If time is of the essence and you have money in your budget for convenience items and hired help, you can get by investing less of your time and energy. Honestly evaluate what your priorities are in terms of what you have to invest in keeping your house looking great. Design your home maintenance routine with these priorities in mind.

- Compare what you say you value to how you actually spend your time. Come clean in terms of what is truly important to you. If having a house that looks great is a priority, plan the time necessary to establish routines that will keep it looking great.

- Set specific, measurable goals to move you in the direction of making your house look and function as you ideally would like. Instead of setting a general goal of having an attractive home, set a more specific goal like repainting your fence or making sure you immediately clean up after every meal.

- Set goals that are realistic. It is better to set a small goal initially and reach it than to set major goals that become so overwhelming you give up before you complete them. If keeping your house looking great is something that seems difficult for you, take it easy and allow yourself some time to change your lifestyle. Perhaps focus your attention on implementing one of these simple ways and achieve that goal. Practice that way of doing things until it becomes a habit, then implement another.

- Aim for balance in your life and protect the balance in the lives of your children. Your goal of having a nice-looking home should not come at the expense of your family being unable to enjoy living in your home. Kids and parents should have time for rest and play, as well as time set aside to keep their home looking great. There should be some times and specific places in which it is okay to make a mess if that is part of something worthwhile for your family.

- Write down your goals and priorities. The process of having to commit these to writing will help you clarify them in your own mind.

39 ✳ Clean As You Go

Most people who keep their homes looking great in a way that seems almost effortless know this simple tool. They clean as they go. Whatever they are doing in their home, they practice cleaning as a routine part of their task. Wherever they are going—from room to room, into the garage or back yard, on their way to get the mail—they have an eye open for anything they can do to keep things looking as they should. Whenever they are on the go and notice something that isn't right, they take action. They pick up gum wrappers, replace empty rolls of toilet tissue, straighten a picture frame without even thinking of it as housework. You can learn to practice cleaning as you go. Here are some simple tips:

- Change your attitude. If you see housework as a grind and put it off until you have to do it, you will end up fighting against yourself when you try to implement a clean-as-you-go philosophy. You need to change your attitude about your home by learning to envision your home as you want it to be. Learn to see every little act as a gift you give yourself and your family to keep the home a nice place to live. Don't give in to feeling like a martyr every time you pick up something another left on the floor. You can choose to have an attitude of love that is demonstrated by each small act you choose to do to clean as you go.

- Teach others to clean as they go. If you begin early with children, they can be taught to take pride in finding things that are out of place and putting things in place. You can even give prizes for times when you notice them doing something to keep your home looking nice that they didn't have to do. Look for these acts and give good "tickets" for a little treat.

- Whenever you are baking or cooking, practice putting away whatever utensils and ingredients you use as soon as you can. It can be overwhelming to wait until you are completely finished with a major job in the kitchen to start cleaning, especially if food has begun to dry.

- Whenever you walk from room to room, don't walk over anything on the floor that you could pick up and dispose of or put back in the room you are headed for. If you are going into a room, look to see if there is anything that needs to go in that direction.

- Whenever you use a sink, notice if it needs to be wiped. If the paper towels are handy (as they should be) it's almost no trouble to grab a paper towel, buff the faucet, and wipe out the sink.

40 * Keep Your Yard Looking Great

Whenever anyone comes to your home, even if it is just to drop something or someone off there, your yard makes an impression. If you want your house to look great, you must have a yard that looks great as well. Here are some ideas for how you can keep your yard looking great with a minimum of time and effort:

- If you find no one in your family seems to have the time or ability to care for your yard, consider hiring someone to help you. You need not spend a fortune either. You can hire a teenager from your neighborhood to cut and edge the lawn on a regular basis. Professional lawn services have a wide variety of services available to suit your needs. Explore the possibilities.

- Change your landscaping to be low maintenance. If you don't want to care for a spacious lawn, consider other low maintenance alternatives, such as rock gardens or filling the area around select plants with rock or wood chips. Talk to someone at your local plant nursery or landscape design company for recommendations. If you choose to use rocks in your landscaping, it is best to use larger rocks. Small rocks tend to get spread around and end up making more work for you. Get advice as to which plants look great without requiring much care, and use these in your yard.

- Use lawn sprinklers on a timer or a drip irrigation system for your lawn, plants, and flowers. This keeps you from having to take time to think about your lawn and to water it yourself. By investing in self-timing devices for lawn care you save yourself a great deal of time and trouble.

- Decorate with flower boxes and bowls of flowers. Ask someone at your local nursery to suggest flowers that would work well for you without requiring much care. The color and beauty of flowers can perk up the appearance of your home dramatically with very little investment of time, energy, or money. God did the work, and you get to enjoy the effect!

- Use bright white paint (or other bright colors that accent your color scheme) to contrast the colors in your yard. Paint scalloped brick lining a flower bed, the pots and flower boxes that hold your flowers and plants, the trim of your house, and other accent pieces.

- Get rid of all eyesores. If you have cars in disrepair, trash cans, and other unsightly objects obscuring the beauty of your home from the exterior, get rid of them. Walk around the block with an objective eye to how the homes appear, then look at your home and ask yourself what needs to be done to make it look neat and clean. Then do whatever needs to be done, or hire someone to do the job. If you have to store something that is unsightly, see if you can store it somewhere out of sight such as your garage or back yard.

41 * Make Your Doorway a Delight

Visitors coming to your home get an impression of your home not only from the way your yard is kept but also from your doorway. This is where they will stand for some period of time with nothing to do but wait and look around. You can make a great impression—indeed make your guests feel welcome—by making your doorway a delight. Here are some ideas you can expand on to keep your doorway looking great:

- Keep it clean. Make sure the walkway to your door, the porch, and the doorway are always clean. Sweep the walk and doorway area regularly. Keep doormats clean by regular sweeping and further cleaning or replacement when necessary.

- Use a doormat as part of your decorating scheme. There are many excellent high-quality doormats that are also beautiful. You may want to select a different decorative doormat for various seasons and holidays: spring, Christmas, Thanksgiving, and so on.

- Keep the critters at bay. Take action to rid your doorway of insects and spiders. Sweep and remove spiderwebs as often as necessary. Check your porch light often and keep it free of spiderwebs and dust. When necessary, spray insect repellant or insecticide, then sweep or hose the area to get rid of the insects and any unpleasant odor.

- Decorate your doorway with a wreath, a painted wood decoration, or an arrangement of dried flowers. This little extra touch adds so much to the warmth of your home and takes so little time and effort.

- Keep your door clean and pretty. If you have windows and curtains or blinds on your front door, make sure these are washed regularly, even though you may forgo regular washing of all your windows. Most families don't wash windows as often as they used to. However, the windows on your door should remain sparkling. Wash them whenever you have the glass cleaner out to clean your living room. Wash or polish your door when you clean your front room. Think of the outside of the door as being part of the room.

- Be creative. I know one family who have taped music connected to their doorbell. They change the tune in keeping with the season. For St. Patrick's Day it plays "When Irish Eyes Are Smiling," at Christmas it plays "Joy to the World," and so on. You can be creative in making your doorway a delight. If guests have had a great experience upon entering your home, you will be making a good impression before they ever step foot inside.

- Create decorative seasonal displays to leave on your doorstep. For example, during the autumn months, place a pumpkin, gourds, Indian corn, and dried leaves near your door. At Christmas, display pots of red and white poinsettias. At Easter, set out a basket of beautifully-colored eggs.

42 * Select What You Will Neglect

President Calvin Coolidge was quoted as saying, "We cannot do everything at once, but we can do something at once." This could become your motto with regard to making your house look great, given the limited amount of time and energy you have to devote to the effort. There was a time in our culture when homemakers were expected to do everything possible to make their homes look great. In some communities, their standing in the eyes of their peers was based on whether their homes would pass the white glove test, whether they wiped down their hot water heater, and how often they stripped and waxed the kitchen floor. Those days are gone (thank goodness).

In our fast-paced society in which many families have both adults working outside the home, societal expectations for perfect housekeeping have slackened. No one should expect you to do everything at once—but you can do *something* at once. The trick is learning to choose what to neglect and knowing when it's time to undertake some of your least favorite chores. Here are a few ideas on the subject:

- Give yourself permission to neglect some things.

- Make a list of acceptable shortcuts: vacuuming without moving the furniture, spot-cleaning the floor rather than mopping, damp mopping rather than scrubbing and waxing, drying out sinks and buffing faucets with a dry paper towel rather than doing thorough bathroom cleaning. Whenever you can take a shortcut without it being obvious, do it.

• Never neglect something that will result in more work for you later, such as neglecting a stain or spill on your carpet. Those things that require immediate care need to be given immediate care.

• Schedule the jobs you don't like into specific time slots on your annual calendar. Make a team effort of these jobs, and give the entire family a good deal of warning so they too can gear up to tackle any unpleasant tasks.

• If you planned to do something for a specific day and find yourself running behind schedule (assuming that you have a plan for your housekeeping chores), look at your overall plan and ask what you can best afford to reschedule. Then give yourself a break and reschedule it for another day.

43 ＊ Plan Your Work and Work Your Plan

In order for home maintenance to be consistent, you need to weave your good intentions into the moments, hours, days, weeks, and months of your life. The best way to do this is to have a plan that integrates your goals for having a great-looking house into your personal and family calendar. If you don't have a calendar system to help you order your life, this may be one reason it is difficult for you to keep your home in order. Order in your home, work, or personal life comes from planning. Take some time to develop a calendar system if you don't already have one. If you do use a calendar system already for work or personal life, be sure to include your housekeeping commitments in this calendar. If you keep it separate it's too easy to overlook in favor of things that seem more urgent or more enjoyable.

Here are some basics to include in your plan:

- Use a planning calendar you can carry with you to organize your time. There are a wide variety of personal organizing systems available at your local stationery or office supply store. Select one that best suits your needs.

- Take time at the beginning of each week to review your plans and add any household tasks that need to be added in consideration of how your house looks at the moment (which is often hard to anticipate when you plan your schedule).

- Plan to give yourself fifteen minutes before you go to bed each night to review your plans for the coming day, including what you will do to keep your house looking great.

- Plan some time for quick home maintenance, training children how to take on more responsibility for themselves, regular family meetings to keep everyone on track, rest, and pursuing other goals.

- Make your calendar system something that works for you, portable, accessible, usable. Feel free to adapt it as you see fit. It is only good if it is used, and you will be more likely to use an organizational system tailored to your personal needs.

- Teach your family members to plan their participation in keeping the house nice into their own goals and plans.

- Have a weekly planning session with each family member. Go over upcoming assignments (from school or work), household responsibilities, activities, appointments, and things they want to do. If it looks as if the number of things to do will be overwhelming, work together to make adjustments before problems have a chance to arise.

- Maintain a calendar in your home to orchestrate the entire family's activities. Then have someone (not necessarily you) coordinate the commitments onto the family calendar kept in a central location.

• Consider taking a class or reading a book that will help you with organization and time management. This is especially helpful if you are not the type of person who keeps to a schedule in other aspects of your life.

44 * Create a Central Intelligence Command Center

Use a family organizational tool to coordinate all the important information your family must have to work together for common goals and plans. This "command center" could be kept in a three-ring binder in a central location such as near the telephone in the kitchen. Your family organizational notebook should include:

- Frequently used telephone numbers. Include the names and numbers of anyone your family calls—your friends, extended family, your children's friends (including their parents' names in case you forget), babysitters, doctors, dentists, emergency numbers such as the poison control hotline, hospital, club leaders, and coaches.

- A copy of the family's monthly and weekly calendar.

- Schedules for all special activities. This could include any changing work schedules, school or college class schedules, sports practice schedules, after-school activities, school lunch menus, and play rehearsals.

- Lists of each person's household responsibilities for the week (in case someone claims to forget). Have family members mark off each responsibility as they finish. This helps in the inspection process. You can look to see if they have checked off an item, then check to see that it's done properly and either praise their work or give corrective instructions about what they need to do to finish the job properly.

- Checklists and instructions for the tasks involved in proper routine cleaning of each room or area in your home. This will keep you from verbally having to repeat these instructions numerous times.

- A section for telephone messages or notes for other family members. Keeping messages in this central location gives messages a better chance of being received. It also allows family members to learn to communicate well in writing. You don't have to limit these just to informational messages. This message center can become a place of praise and congratulations shared by the whole family. When you take the lead, your children may find fun in building one another up.

- A section to hold business cards you may need.

- A section for suggestions. These could be suggestions of fun places to visit as a family, ways to keep the house looking great, solutions for shared family problems, and so on. Go over the suggestion section of the notebook at family meetings. Be sure that all suggestions are acknowledged and appreciated even if they are not adopted.

• A section for listing things to buy on the next trip to the store.

45 ✳ Listen While You Work

Admittedly, housework can be boring. And being bored while you clean house can slow you down. Listening to something while you work can keep you from being bored and make your time cleaning house more personally rewarding. Note—it's listening, not watching, that is being recommended. You usually need to be free to move around quickly while you are doing housework. Getting glued to the television can distract you and keep you planted in one spot when you should be moving. It's great to do something to make your house look better while you are watching TV. It's not good to watch TV when you have scheduled time to clean. Here are some ideas about what to listen to while you work:

- Get a portable tape player that attaches to your clothes or belt. In this way you can listen to your favorite tapes while you work. Try to find tapes that are upbeat. Music you enjoy with a lively tempo or motivational tapes that inspire you are great. Music and motivational tapes can change your attitude, and that can actually affect how well and how fast you do your work.

- Use your time cleaning to get an education. There are many educational programs now available on audio. If you are of the opinion that cleaning is a mindless activity, use the time for educational purposes—learn a foreign language, study economics, whatever piques your interest.

- Experience a good book. Many best-selling books are now available on audiotape. You can purchase these at most bookstores, rent them, or check them out at your local library.

- Listen to the radio. Find a station that plays music you enjoy and give yourself the pleasure of enjoying your favorite tunes while you work. If your family doesn't want to hear the radio while you do, consider using a portable radio with earphones.

- If the family is working together, select some music that everyone can agree on as being acceptable (granted, this is not an easy task for some families), and play music on a stereo system throughout the house.

- Encourage other family members to listen while they work. There are great audiotapes for children, including sound tracks from Disney movies, stories, and song collections. These can be found at children's bookstores and some educational toy stores. Children can use your portable tape player, or get them a tape player designed for children.

- Students can use a tape recorder to turn time spent on routine chores into study time. One effective way of studying—especially when there is set material to be memorized—is to record the material on audiotape. Tape yourself asking a question; then wait several seconds before giving the answer. While you are doing routine chores, listen to the tape and try to answer the questions before the tape gives you the correct answer.

46 ∗ Create Places Designed to Meet Needs

The design and upkeep of your home should be planned to accommodate the needs of your family on a daily basis. When your home is functional there will be built-in motivation to keep things in order, since leaving things out of order will directly affect whether or not needs are met. Each place designed around the needs of your family should have all necessary materials within reach. Here are some places you might consider creating within your home:

- A place for study and homework. This would include good lighting, a solid clean writing surface, pens, pencils, markers, eraser, correction fluid, a stapler, and paper clips. It might also include a computer and reference books.

- A place for snacking and meals (the way your family has them). You may want to create a sandwich center near your refrigerator so everything necessary for making sandwiches is handy. You could also include items like paper plates, trays, napkins, and a sponge (to wipe up when they are finished).

- A place for entertaining friends of the family, your friends and your children's friends. Consider your preferences for entertaining, the kinds of things you enjoy doing (playing games, conversing, watching movies together), and then design a place that has what you need within easy reach. If you have friends who usually bring their children to play with your children while you entertain the adults, plan how you will coexist with the children. This may mean you want to designate another room as a video game room for the children (or whatever their interests are), which will allow the adults to enjoy their time together.

- A place for family meals and formal dining (if that suits your needs). Have dinnerware, china, stemware, place mats, napkins, and other table setting materials easily accessible.

- A place for children to play. There needs to be someplace in your home where children feel free to get their toys out and play. Design it in a way that makes it easy to put toys away when play time is over.

- A place for each individual in your family to develop at his stage of development. Careful planning with the developmental stages of children in mind can reduce conflict and the mess that can come from the conflict. For example, an adolescent daughter will need some privacy. If you give her a place that is protected from the curious, often rummaging, hands of younger siblings, she will take better care of her place (which serves her need for privacy). She will have more personal pride in keeping her room nice if she knows little brother is not going to come in and destroy it. On the other hand, if little brother is two or three, he will need a place where there are things he can touch and explore without getting into trouble.

- A place within your refrigerator just for leftovers.

- A place for things people promise to put away in a minute. Just make sure the "in a minute" place is cleaned out before bedtime each night.

- Have a key holder near the entryway to your home.

47 * Set Rules and Boundaries

Boundaries and rules should be set for the safety, security, and well-being of the people who live in your home. When your family and those who visit your home understand the boundaries, they will be able to feel comfortable there because they will know exactly what to expect. Here are some guidelines for establishing rules and boundaries for your home:

- Reevaluate rules and boundaries as your family grows and as life changes. With every major change (a new baby, a new job, a new schedule at work, a child reaching high school), rules and boundaries should be evaluated and adapted to meet the changing needs of your family.

- Make sure everyone knows what activities are allowed in which rooms or areas of your house. If snacking is only allowed in the kitchen, make that clear. If children are allowed to run in the play room but not in any other room, let them know it. Ask yourself what behavior is unacceptable for each room of your house. Then clearly communicate these boundaries to all family members.

- If you have a pool or other backyard equipment that could pose a danger, post rules for correct use of the area in writing and make sure the rules are read and understood by anyone using the area for the first time.

- Make sure your children's friends understand the rules and boundaries for your home. If these are explained in a friendly way at a time when they are not already being violated, they should make the children feel more comfortable there.

- If the rules or boundaries are violated, be consistent in your response. If your children's friends violate the rules, take responsibility for explaining the consequences and enforcing the rules. Don't put your child in the awkward position of having to enforce family rules while you are around.

- Only have as many rules as are necessary for the protection and safety of your home and the people who share it.

Here are some basic rules to get you thinking:

- Put things back where they belong when finished using them. If you get it out, you are responsible for putting it back.

- You are responsible for getting your dirty clothes into the hamper.

- Show respect for other people's possessions. Do not hurt them or treat them carelessly.

- Do not break, hit, kick, or throw things in the house.

- Use quiet inside voices when inside. No shouting or screaming indoors.

- Household jobs and responsibilities are assigned according to age and ability.

- Jobs may be traded and negotiated, especially during weeks or seasons when demands elsewhere are pressing. For example, when adults or working children have a pressing deadline at work, when children have a major project due at school, or during sports season when the child is expending great amounts of energy, some allowances will be made.

48 * Plan to Make Mealtimes Quick and Easy

Much of the work around the home is associated with meals. Cooking, serving, and cleaning up after meals takes up time and creates some degree of mess continually, several times each day. If you find ways to streamline meal preparation and clean-up, you will make a significant impact on keeping your house looking great. Here are some ideas of how you can do this:

- Learn to use the microwave for cooking as well as reheating things. When using the microwave oven, be sure to follow recipes exactly. The principles of microwave cooking are different from cooking with conventional ovens. You need to become familiar with these principles before improvising. If you experiment according to conventional principles of cooking, you may have a mess to clean up and another meal to make when yours explodes!

- Experiment with recipes for quick, easy-to-prepare meals found in most women's and home magazines.

- Eat out occasionally.

- Clean up as you cook. Rinse pots and pans, put things in the dishwasher, and put away ingredients as you use them.

- Take a cooking class that focuses on quick and easy meals. Often people get into a rut of cooking only those things they feel confident cooking. If you gain confidence cooking meals that are quick and easy, you will be more likely to serve them regularly to your family.

- Use a slow cooker or Crockpot so your meal can be cooking while you do something else.

- If you love the smell and taste of homemade bread but don't have the time necessary to bake it, consider getting a bread-making oven. These ovens are designed to do all the work for you. All you do is put in the ingredients and follow simple directions. The oven does the mixing, kneading, and baking. Your family does the eating.

- Choose dishes that are dishwasher-safe.

- Use a dishwasher.

- Organize your refrigerator, freezer, and pantry to give you easy access to the ingredients you need.

- Supplement home-cooked meals with frozen meals. There are a wide variety of frozen foods on the market today that are both nutritious and delicious. There are toaster waffles, microwave-ready pancakes, and all sorts of frozen breakfast foods that can be prepared in moments. There are even frozen dinners designed to meet the portion requirements, nutritional needs, and preferences of children. These frozen foods are great time-savers and may also give you a break from your typical menu items.

49 ✳ Use Silk or Dried Plants and Flowers

Authentic-looking silk and artificial plants and flowers add beauty without requiring the amount of care real plants need. They stay beautiful year round without shedding leaves or bringing dirt into your home. They don't need to be watered, so there is no chance of having messy spills to clean up. Using silk plants and other artificial plants can be a supplement to the real plants you love or a substitute, depending on your preference.

Silk plants come in a wide variety of types. You can get palms, hanging plants, flowering plants, even bushes that look like the real thing. Make sure you get high-quality silk plants that don't look obviously artificial. If you really want to throw people as to whether your plants are the real thing, put a few dead leaves from the same kind of plant in with your silk plant. It works! You may also want to use silk plants up high, on ledges and hanging from the ceiling and only have live plants lower down where they come under closer scrutiny.

Here are some tips for keeping your silk plants looking great:

- You can dust them with a dusting cloth or feather duster treated with antistatic spray or dusting spray.

- You can use a blow dryer to get the dust off before you vacuum.

- When you need to clean your silk plants take them outside, hose them off with your garden hose, and let them dry in the sunshine.

- Dried plants and flowers are also becoming popular decorating items. You will find a wide variety of wall hangings, wreaths, baskets, even furniture crafted from twigs, dried flowers, and other dried plants. Another variation is bunches of dried flowers hanging upside down and tied with bows or ribbons. If you like this style of decorator items, enjoy them. They are very easy to care for because they don't really need to be dusted regularly. Some people claim that the dust just adds to their quaint appeal. Should you want to get the dust off, just run your blow dryer on a cool/low setting and blow the dust away. Then vacuum and dust the surrounding area.

50 * Practice the Fine Art of Hiding

There are occasions when you don't have enough time to do the kind of thorough cleaning you might opt for under ideal circumstances. An announcement of unexpected company, having friends over thirty minutes after you arrive home from work, or discovering that little hands have been busy creating messes as fast as you have been cleaning them are all examples of times when you may need to resort to practicing the fine art of hiding.

Here are some ideas of how you can use this strategy to make your house look great (to the unsuspecting eye) in a hurry:

- Close a door. If company is due to arrive in an hour and you realize there is no way to get the entire house in tip-top shape, it's okay to consolidate your disorder into one room and keep that room off limits to guests.

- Keep one cabinet or storage space in your home free to use as a hideaway. Whenever you need to do a quick pick-up and don't have time to put things where they belong, temporarily put them in your hideaway. Be sure to take time to empty the hideaway within twenty-four hours.

- Draw shower curtains or close the shower door if you haven't finished cleaning the tub and/or tile.

- Use candlelight for camouflage. If you are entertaining during evening hours and are concerned that your home is not polished to spotless perfection or free of dust, try having a candlelight dinner. Candlelight gives a charming effect, and your guests need never know that you had a hidden agenda.

- Keep dirt in disguise. Use medium colors for decorating purposes. Light and dark colors tend to show dirt more, especially on floor coverings. If you have carpet in areas where people eat, assume there will be spills and plan ahead by choosing patterns that are multicolored. These more readily hide stains. For tile floors and countertops, choose grout in dark colors to hide the dirt.

51 * Motivate Yourself and Others

As with most things in life, when it comes to keeping your house looking great, attitude makes all the difference. If you can learn to motivate yourself and members of your household to keep a positive attitude toward the work of keeping your home looking great, you will be miles ahead. Here are some tips and ideas to help you use motivation as a powerful housekeeping tool:

- List and talk about the benefits of staying on track with your plans to keep your home looking great. Ask your family members what they most enjoy when the house is well kept. Appeal to the benefits they value. Some benefits might be feeling a sense of pride (or avoiding embarrassment) when friends visit, having an easier time finding things, being able to relax, and enjoying the beauty.

- Look over your plans the night before cleaning up and visualize the immediate benefits you will receive if you keep your commitment to do what needs to be done around the house.

- Make each job visible with a touch of flair, each person's own signature that tells everyone that a job has been done and who has done it. One person may leave a special scent in the bathroom after he has finished his daily routine cleaning. When the kitchen is finished you may want to leave a single fresh flower in a bud vase on the table. When the bedding is changed, leave mints on the pillows to remind those benefiting from your work that you have done it with love. When family members have ways of expressing themselves as they do their work and receive recognition for what they have done, they will maintain their motivation to do jobs that otherwise may seem thankless.

- Always be sure to praise and thank those who do their jobs well rather than taking their cooperation for granted and then adding more work to their load (because they have shown they can handle it).

- Give recognition for jobs well done. You can use a star chart for children, giving them a star for each chore completed. You can also give verbal recognition before the other members of your family or household whenever someone has done a good job. A word of recognition costs you nothing, and yet the return on your investment will be significant.

- Teach family members to appreciate the efforts of others. At family meetings, ask members to mention one thing they noticed someone else do to keep the house looking great that they appreciate.

- You may want to use small prizes and incentives to keep things moving. You could have a drawing for a small prize at the end of each week. Enter only the names of those who accomplished their housekeeping goals/plans for the week. Or you may want to give a special treat for family members who complete their weekly commitments rather than threatening punishment for not doing a chore. A few weeks of missing out on a special treat when everyone else gets one can have a dramatic effect.

• Finally, have a vision and share your vision. Do you and the members of your household have a clear vision of how nice your home could be if you all worked together to keep it up? If you lack vision, you will have a difficult time inspiring anyone. Here's one way you can get and share the vision of a great-looking home: Plan a time to get your entire home looking its absolute best at one time. This means having every room clean, all laundry done and put away, and each area of your home in order. Then give a tour. Pretend it's a home tour and guide your family through each room, praising how great it looks. They will know how great it feels. Then explain that you are intent on having your family learn skills that will allow you all to enjoy living in a home that routinely stays looking nice. Although you will not necessarily keep your house looking that great all the time, they will have the vision to aim for. It's much like working a puzzle. If you have the picture on the cover of the box in mind, you are motivated to put the pieces together. If your family has the vision for how nice your home can be, they will become more motivated to put in their piece.

In closing, I'd like to say a few words to those who have never known the pleasure of living in a house that looks great most of the time. Perhaps you grew up in a home where things were always in disarray. Maybe you see yourself as a messy person because you grew up in such surroundings or never learned the skills and systems that would allow you to live in a great-looking home.

The truth is that you can change. You can change your attitude about yourself and realize that you are not destined to be a messy person. You can learn new skills and habits that will transform your surroundings. Most important, by making changes to keep your house looking great, you can change your self-image and enhance the self-esteem of every member of your family. When you live in a home that looks great, you can't help but feel better about yourself and your life.

If this is new for you, don't try to do it all at once. That will only discourage you and perhaps even convince you that people like you can't keep your house looking great. Instead, take it slowly. Perhaps you will want to institute one suggestion a week over the course of the coming year. Take your time, applaud your progress, and don't give up. You and your family deserve to live in beautiful and orderly surroundings. Here's wishing you all the best!

III. Simplify Your Life

*To my wife, Tricia—thou excellest them all!
And to our friends, Jerome and Dorothy—fellow
pilgrims on the narrow way*

■ Contents

Cultivate Your Spirit

Make Peace with Your Enemies

Simplify Your Finances

Do It Yourself

Don't Do It Yourself

■■ Introduction

*Our life is frittered away by detail. An honest man
has hardly need to count more than his ten fingers,
or in extreme cases he may add his ten toes, and
lump the rest. Simplicity, simplicity, simplicity!*
                                    —Henry David Thoreau

Our lives get more complex every day.
How many of us haven't longed to drop
out altogether? We read about men and women
who have left high-paying careers and moved to
the country to find a higher quality of life, and
something tugs at all of us to get out, to return to a
simpler life-style.

Even the little things in our lives are burdensome. Most of us still can't figure out how to record a show on the VCR. By the time we learn how
to use it, it will be obsolete!

The volume of choices we face is overwhelming.
There are fifty-three channels on our TV cable system, forty kinds of soap to wash our dishes, and
hundreds of styles of clothing to choose from.

We're bombarded with information. The average
person sees several thousand advertising messages every day. There are more words in the average Sunday newspaper than in the entire Bible.

Information changes so quickly that an encyclopedia is out of date by the time it's printed.

I have good news. There is a way out of this complexity short of moving to the backwoods in Maine. It's possible to simplify our lives. It's possible to find an island of peace in the midst of this frantic world. People have always faced this issue. It's harder today than it's ever been, but the principles passed down from earlier generations still work.

This book offers practical information. It's not a philosophical treatise about simplicity. I'm a businessman, with all the demands of balancing family, church, career, and community. My wife and I have worked hard for the last ten years to simplify our lives. Through trial and error, we've had some success. The suggestions in this book have worked for us.

Most of the ideas are simple. (I wouldn't be very consistent if I gave complex suggestions to simplify your life!) But just because the ideas are simple doesn't mean they're all easy to incorporate into your life. Complexity is addicting. Slowing down, even though you desire it, is a challenge. If you have eyes to see the problem and the will to make changes, the suggestions here will work for you. Once you get started, the joy of a simpler life will be all the motivation you need to keep going. May you find greater peace and joy than you ever thought possible!

Develop Habits of Rest and Reflection

The driven person can never lead a simple life.
Liberating yourself from drivenness is the
essential first step.

1 ■ Get Enough Sleep

Fatigue makes cowards of us all.
—Vince Lombardi

Background Some experts now believe that adults need between eight and ten hours of sleep per night. The average adult gets seven hours.

Think about the days before electric lights and television. People had little to do after dark. Families sat near the fire and talked. I'm sure it didn't take long to get sleepy. Most people were in bed a few hours after sundown. The body's rhythms were therefore dictated by the length of the day. In the summer, they would be up early and work hard until late at night. But for most of the year, eight to ten hours were probably a normal night's sleep.

Think about what happens to you on vacation. That can indicate what your body is trying to tell you. I usually continue my normal sleeping pattern the first few days. By the fourth or fifth day, I sleep an extra hour or two. If it's a long vacation, I sleep ten hours at night and even take a nap at midday by the second week.

If our bodies really do need eight to ten hours of sleep, how do we get by on seven? We make up the difference with adrenaline. But we pay the price in fatigue and reduced effectiveness.

Action   If you are tired most of the time, there is only one solution: sleep more. If this applies to you, getting more sleep is the first step toward simplifying your life.

That's easier said than done, I know. How can you afford to sleep more since you have so much to do? Throughout the rest of this book, the other 51 ways should show you how to find more time. But begin now to give yourself permission to sleep. Many of us feel guilty about sleeping. That's silly. Our bodies are designed to need sleep, just as we need air and water. We don't feel guilty taking the air and water we need.

For those of us on a job schedule, it's usually not possible to sleep later in the morning. We must go to bed earlier. If you watch TV in the evenings, turn it off and allow your mind to wind down earlier. Television and electric lights artificially stimulate us. Long after earlier generations would have been in bed, we are in front of the TV, unaware that the body is telling us it's tired. Try taking a hot bath to help you relax. If you are married, you and your spouse can rub each other's back in bed.

Try going to bed fifteen minutes earlier. If it works, add another fifteen minutes. Consider whether you have more energy the next day. You may miss out on a chunk of time each day, but you'll more than make up for it in increased energy!

2 ▪▪ Have a Rest Day

The Sabbath was made for man.

—Mark 2:27

Background If you are a Christian or a Jew, you know the concept of a Sabbath. God decreed that everyone must rest one day each week. He considered it so important that He made it one of the Ten Commandments. No work could be done on the Sabbath.

Why did God establish a rest day? Because it's good for us. It fits our natural rhythms. Our bodies need times of rest. Constant activity, day after day with no breaks, is like music without any rests.

It's an established medical fact that people with Type A personalities, those who have trouble resting, have more heart attacks, high blood pressure, ulcers, and a host of other problems.

We also benefit spiritually from a rest day because it's an act of faith to stop working. We have faith that there is One who will take care of us, that we needn't strive seven days a week. We say, "God, I trust You with the consequences of stopping to rest today."

Action It doesn't matter what day you choose to rest; it's just important that you take off a day. For most of us, Sunday is a good day. We work five days for an employer, Saturday is the day we catch up on personal business, and Sunday is the most natural day to take it easy.

Starting this habit takes discipline. I began it two years ago when I had a full-time job and was consulting for extra income. I could do my consulting work at home, and I usually chose Sunday to do it. I was making good money, but I was increasingly stressed. I knew I had to change something. My quality of life was deteriorating rapidly.

I made a commitment to try to have a rest day.

At first, I was obsessed on Sunday morning with thoughts of all I could achieve that day. I kept reminding myself that it was my day to rest, and I asked God to help me trust Him with my unfinished work. After church, I would read, take a nap, take a walk with Tricia, go on an outing at the beach, help cook a nice meal—anything that was relaxing.

Now, this habit is one of the most rewarding disciplines of my life. I still find time to do occasional consulting on a day other than Sunday. In fact, I don't feel I have lost any time. My outlook on life is much more focused, my energy is higher, and I have learned a vital lesson about my natural rhythms. I have lost nothing; I have gained a higher quality of life.

3 ■ Get Away from It All

He that can take rest is better than he that can take cities.

—Ben Franklin

Background Even if we get enough sleep and have a rest day each week, we still need longer breaks. The right kind of vacation refreshes us physically, emotionally, and spiritually.

There are two kinds of vacations: the relaxing kind and the *other* kind. Tricia and I like to go places we have never been before, and my business has made it possible for us to travel all over the world. We discovered some years ago that traveling around Europe or Asia for two weeks is not relaxing. That may sound obvious, but we had many disappointing vacations before we figured it out. We still love to do it, but we will take no more than one of these trips every year or two.

I've seen many families take car trips or camping trips or go to someplace like Disneyland, and they invariably come home tired. There's nothing wrong with that kind of vacation if you recognize it for what it is and schedule time to recover before returning to work.

Tricia and I now plan at least one week a year for a truly relaxing vacation. We go to one location and stay there. We choose a place that allows us outdoor recreation—fishing or hiking—but all from a comfortable home base. One of our favorite spots is a friend's cabin on a lake in northern Minnesota.

We've even discovered how to make an overseas trip relaxing. We choose one place, such as a mountain village in Switzerland, and we stay there a whole week, hiking during the day and enjoying the local food at night.

Rejuvenating vacations have helped me make some of the most important decisions in my life. I made my biggest career move after spending a week in a Swiss mountain village. I don't think I could have made the decision any other way. I needed the clarity of being completely alone with my wife, utterly rested, and away from all the pressures of daily living.

Action   Take your vacations. If you are someone who feels pride in not taking vacations, you are missing some of the best times of life.

Plan your vacations with the clear understanding of what kind each is to be. Make sure at least one vacation this year is the rejuvenating kind.

If your vacation is likely to leave you tired, come home a few days before you must return to work. Give yourself time to rest, or you're likely to get depressed when you have to go back to work.

Save for vacations. You can't have fun if you're worrying about money. And you don't need to spend a lot to have a good experience. Ask friends for suggestions. One of them just might have a cabin in Minnesota that you can use!

4 ∷ Take Miniretreats

To see a world in a grain of sand
And a heaven in a wild flower,
Hold infinity in the palm of your hand
And eternity in an hour.

—William Blake

Background The goal of rest days and vacations is to ultimately bring the peace we feel during our times of rest into our busy times. When I first began working to find more peace in my daily life, the contrast between the times of rest and my daily life was huge. I felt like two different people. No matter how refreshed I was on vacation, the feeling evaporated by 9:00 A.M. on my first day back to work. That is no longer true. I have learned to carry some of it with me all the time.

One way to help you carry a peaceful attitude into your daily routines is to find times for miniretreats throughout the day.

Action A miniretreat is anything that slows you down, anything that brings enjoyment or gives you perspective.

Find some activities that cause your heart rate to slow just a bit. Set aside times to reflect on what you are doing. Look for the good things in life, and pause to enjoy them.

Have lunch alone occasionally. As a busy executive, I believe this is one of the best things I do for myself. I used to have lunch appointments every day. Almost by accident, I discovered that taking a magazine, leaving the office, and having lunch by myself made my whole day. I was cheerier all afternoon. The time alone brought perspective on the decisions I needed to make or the meetings I had that afternoon. Soon I was refusing to take all but the most important lunch appointments.

You can take a miniretreat almost anywhere. When I'm traveling, I try to avoid my tendency to work or read every minute. Sometimes I'll sit a few minutes and watch people. Sometimes I'll look out the window of the airplane and reflect on my life from the perspective of 32,000 feet.

If you live near mountains, stop what you are doing from time to time and look at them. Go outside tonight and look at the stars, no matter where you live. If you have flowers in your yard, take a moment to stop and smell them. (There's a lot of truth in some clichés!)

Complexity and busyness are like a spiral. The busier we get, the less time we have to pause and reflect. And the less time we pause, the more we take on. We move faster and faster, and we lose the perspective we need to keep our lives focused and simple. Miniretreats are one powerful way to regularly step out of the spiral.

Get Rid of Distractions

A distraction is anything that takes time and doesn't contribute to long-term goals, personal growth, or a peaceful heart. The trouble is, we enjoy many distractions.

5 ■ Stop the Newspaper

I am sure that I never read any memorable news in a newspaper . . . to a philosopher all news, as it is called, is gossip, and they who edit and read it are old women over their tea. Yet not a few are greedy after this gossip.

—Henry David Thoreau

Background The problem with the newspaper is that it comes first thing every day. It arrives on the doorstep and announces that we must do something with it before we can leave the house. It cries out to be read before the news is no longer news.

Thoreau couldn't understand why people would read the newspaper. He is as right today as he was then: it is primarily gossip, not news. Almost everything in the newspaper is gossip about people, about what *might* happen, or about some tragic events that we'd be just as well off not to know. Thoreau wrote,

If we read of one man robbed, or murdered, or killed by accident, or one house burned, or one vessel wrecked, or one steamboat blown up, or one cow run over on the Western Railroad, or one mad dog killed, or one lot of grasshoppers in the winter,—we never need read of another. One is enough. If you are acquainted with the

principle, what do you care for a myriad in-
stances and applications?

I'm not against staying informed. I subscribe to a
weekly news magazine. I used to spend several
hours a week reading the paper. I can browse
through my news magazine in fifteen minutes and
know everything I need to know about the world.

There are more words in the Sunday *Los Angeles
Times* or *New York Times* than in many books. Ask
yourself, How much of real importance do I find in
the newspaper?

Action   Cancel your newspaper subscription. If
you want to read the paper occasionally, buy it
from the newsstand. That will assure it doesn't
crowd out more important things. If you buy it
only when you have the time and the inclination,
you'll soon find you read it far less often.

6 ■ Turn Off the Television

Amusing Ourselves to Death
—Title of Neil Postman's book about the effects of TV on our culture

Background You knew this was coming, didn't you? Television is one of the most troubling aspects of our culture. Children today spend thousands of hours watching TV before they even enter school. People in the average household watch seven or eight hours per day. And most of the programming is the entertainment equivalent of junk food.

I grew up on a steady diet of TV. I watched it all —"The Ed Sullivan Show," "Leave It to Beaver," and slightly less classic shows such as "My Mother the Car." I went on into adulthood and graduated to "60 Minutes" and "thirtysomething."

Four years ago, several of our friends decided to cancel their cable TV subscriptions. I was surprised. It was like pulling the life-support system out of the home. Where they live among the mountains, they can't receive any channels without cable.

Tricia and I watched their experiment with interest. Their children fretted mightily at first. But soon they were staying outside and playing with their friends. They were riding their bikes. They had virtually forgotten all about TV within three months. When Christmas came, the children wanted clothes and dolls instead of the latest electronic gadgets. The realization of the effect of advertising on our friends' children convinced Tricia and me to do the same.

At first I was fidgety around the time of my favorite shows. But we began to have exceptional evenings—unlike anything we'd ever experienced. We'd linger over dinner, talking about important topics. We'd listen to our favorite music or read books. We'd hold our young children. As an extra benefit, by canceling our cable subscription, we saved enough money to go out for dinner every other month.

I must admit that we still have a TV, but we only receive two channels. We often rent movies on the weekends, and we watch TV when there is something special like the Olympics. But I am now amazed when I recall how much time I used to waste watching that silly thing. And when I see the promotions for the newest situation comedies, I can hardly believe that sensible adults will waste even a half hour of their lives watching such ridiculous shows. It's like living on Kool-Aid while ignoring life's banquet of experiences.

Action   I know that turning off the TV will be difficult for most people in today's culture. I think most of us must go cold turkey. Try it for a week. Agree to watch no TV. See what happens. Don't judge it by the first few days because it's like withdrawing from a drug. If you feel conviction as you read this section, call the cable company before the notion passes. And be prepared to fend off an onslaught from your children.

If abstinence is too much for you, try reviewing what you watch in the upcoming week. Ask your family, "What value did we get from watching this show?"; "Did it teach us something?"; "Did it uplift us, inspire us, or help us in any way?"; "Would we recommend that our friends watch it?"

Over time, cut out those shows that do nothing for you. And avoid leaving the TV on just because you've got nothing better to do. If there's an hour between your favorite shows, turn off the TV and talk or read. See if you can't wean your children and yourselves from spending so much unproductive time in front of the TV.

There's more to life than watching someone else's made-up experiences. Embark on your own real adventures instead.

7 ▪▪ Limit Magazines, and Read Great Books Instead

How many a man has dated a new era in his life from the reading of a book.
—Henry David Thoreau

Background Like the newspaper, magazines can be intrusive. We know that if we don't read this week's news magazine or this month's food magazine, another one will soon be upon us. We end up reading a magazine before tackling a much more important task because the magazine is dated. I've found myself attacking a stack of magazines just to get through them when I'd really rather be doing something else.

I can think of perhaps two or three memorable magazine articles I've read in my entire life. I tore those articles from the magazines and still have them today. The other five or six hundred articles I've read are now in a landfill somewhere.

My shelves, in contrast, are full of books that have affected my life. *Anna Karenina* awakened me to the deceitfulness of the human heart and vividly portrayed the destructive effects of an extramarital affair. I cannot see a poor person without feeling the sympathy that Dominique La-Pierre's *City of Joy* evoked for a poor Indian rickshaw driver. And as you may have guessed,

Thoreau's *Walden* has had such a profound influence on me that I have nearly worn out my first copy. How much time have I wasted plowing through stacks of magazines while I've virtually ignored the great classics of world literature at the local library?

Action If you subscribe to more magazines than you can comfortably keep up with, stop some of them. If you like to read, read books, especially classics. If a book has been around some time and is famous, there's usually a good reason for it—it has influenced many people.

One caution is still in order. Books can complicate your life, too. If you're the kind of person who has several books going at once, try reading only one at a time.

8 ■■ Stop the Noise

There can be no very black melancholy to him who lives in the midst of Nature and has his senses still.
—Henry David Thoreau

Background Few places left on earth are not polluted by human-made noise. Tricia and I recently took a backpacking trip through Yosemite. In very remote wilderness, we were dismayed to discover that a jet flew overhead every twenty minutes, day and night. We have been in remote areas of Africa where there is truly no noise other than wind and birds. It's almost eerie to a person who lives in the U.S.

I don't believe that our brains were built to withstand so much noise. It's a source of stress—a background kind of stress that we don't even notice. Worse yet, we contribute to it by unnecessarily surrounding ourselves with noise. We have radios in our cars, radios in our homes, and radios to strap to us when we aren't near the car or the house. We turn on the TV and leave it on while we're in another room.

This noise keeps our minds off the things that really matter. I discovered some time ago that if I drove home from work in silence, I processed the happenings of the day. I thought about what went well and what didn't. I thought about the motives behind people's actions. I thought about what I needed to do the next day. By the time I arrived home, I was ready to put the day behind me. Tricia noticed the difference in me within a few weeks. She said I seemed less preoccupied in the evenings. I now see that when I listened to the radio all the way home, I never processed the day. Thoughts about work kept popping into my mind all evening.

In the past, people sought quiet solitude in the desert or the mountains, and they didn't have anywhere near the amount of noise that we do! We have lost an appreciation of silence.

Action Stop the noise whenever you can. Try riding in the car with the radio off. Be aware of what comes to your mind, and process those things. Ask yourself why they came to mind: Do I need to analyze a situation? Is there a decision I need to make?

Don't turn on the TV if you aren't watching it.

Find times when you can be alone and sit quietly. I often hike into the mountains alone. I use the time to pray and to reflect on my life and any decisions I face. Even a half hour can be greatly refreshing.

9 ■ Experiment with Peace

Sometimes, in a summer morning, having taken my accustomed bath, I sat in my sunny doorway from sunrise till noon, rapt in a revery, amidst the pines and hickories and sumachs, in undisturbed solitude and stillness, while the birds sang around or flitted noiseless through the house, until by the sun falling in at my west window, or the noise of some traveller's wagon on the distant highway, I was reminded of the lapse of time. I grew in those seasons like corn in the night, and they were far better than any work of the hands would have been. They were not time subtracted from my life, but so much over and above my usual allowance.

—Henry David Thoreau

Background In our search for simplicity, we need to run counter to our contemporaries and actually get rid of some things that others are striving for. Until we try being without something—not watching TV, turning off the radio in the car, or doing without a second car—we won't know whether it's good for us or not.

The assumption that more things, more friends, and more activities are good for us is flatly wrong. We all have limited time, and unless we focus that time toward truly important things, we will find ourselves wasting vast quantities of it. Our lives will be so full on the outside that we will be empty on the inside. And the worst part of it is this: the more complex our lives become, the less we are aware of it.

Action Cultivate an awareness of your inner peace. Run small experiments in your life, the goal being to measure the effect of a change on your sense of peace. Try going without some thing or activity. Ask yourself, Do I have more or less peace?

Try changing your schedule and consider what it does for your inner peace. Try doing something in the evening if your mornings are terribly busy.

I found a different way to drive to work. It was a less direct route. It took me five minutes longer. But it improved the quality of my life. It avoided the freeway and its associated headaches. The route took me along the foothills of our local mountains. In the evenings, the sun turns the mountains golden, and I have enjoyed many a beautiful drive home after a hard day's work. In short, I changed my perspective on the drive home from looking only at the commuting time to evaluating how I felt.

I avoided buying a computer until long after all my friends owned one. I finally bought one, and in this case, a complex electronic gadget has simplified my life. Writing with a word processing program and paying my bills with a financial package save me many hours and truly simplify the tasks. Experiment with changes in your life, and evaluate whether peace and simplicity are the outcomes.

10 ▪▪ Know Where Your Time Goes

Do not squander time, for that is the stuff life is made of.

—Ben Franklin

Background Do you know where your time goes? Probably the oldest management advice is simply to know where your time goes. For decades, management experts have advised busy executives to track their time in fifteen-minute blocks for one or two weeks. The advice is excellent for everyone. Most people are quite surprised to discover how they actually spend their time.

Action For one or two weeks, track your time in fifteen-minute increments. Keep a sheet near you, and update it whenever you happen to remember. Do it at least every few hours, or you're apt to forget what you did earlier that day.

When you've completed the exercise, group your activities into reasonable categories—attending meetings, reading, doing chores, talking with the family, going to church, eating meals, and so on—and add up the time in each category.

Then ask yourself,

- Was that activity worthwhile?
- Did it contribute to my goals?

- Did it help someone else?

- Did I have enough time for rest and reflection?

- Did I invest any time in my personal growth?

- Are there things I did that I should delegate to others?

- Are there blocks of time I wasted?

Knowing *where* you spend your time is the first step toward improving *how* you spend it.

Focus Your Life

What do you want from life?

11 ■ Accept Yourself

To thine own self be true.
—William Shakespeare

Background In all the world, there's only one you. No one has your exact genes or your same experiences. The combination is truly unique.

One of the sad facts of life is that few of us are content with ourselves as we are. We think, *If only I looked like her . . . ; If only I made as much money as he does . . . ; If only I could sing like that . . . ; If only I could get a break like she did . . . ;* and on and on.

Action Accept yourself. Life will never be simple until you do. That doesn't mean you should stop growing or give up trying to change bad habits. It means you should stop trying to be someone you're not. If your parents wanted you to be an opera singer and you can't carry a tune, stop feeling guilty. If you don't have the energy to raise two kids, hold down a job, and write a great novel, stop pushing yourself. The novel can wait until the kids grow up.

For many of us, accepting ourselves is very difficult. We may struggle with deep issues that arise from childhood. We may need to seek professional help. As an adult child of alcoholic parents, I can testify to the value of professional help in uncovering some of the hidden drivers in my life.

Take a few minutes to write a description of yourself. Answer these questions:

- What are my strengths?

- What do others say about me?

- What are my weaknesses? Can I accept these weaknesses?

- What unique experiences have I had? (Even negative ones can be used to help others. My current employer likes to hire people who have had at least one business failure. Humility helps in the consulting business!)

- What would I like to change about myself? Are these things reasonable?

- What circumstances dictate my situation right now (for example, having small children)?

Ask your spouse or a friend to review the list with you. Use this self-description to begin accepting yourself.

12 ■ Know Your Values

I went to the woods because I wished to live deliberately, . . . and not, when I came to die, to discover that I had not lived. I wanted to live deep and suck out all the marrow of life.
—Henry David Thoreau

Background What is most important to you in life? Is there anything you'd be willing to die for? Is there anything you feel passionate about?

The things that mean the very most to us represent our values. If I'm willing to die to protect my family, family is obviously a very high value in my life. If I'm willing to die for my country, patriotism is a high value.

Similarly, each of us is willing to invest time in certain things. A friend of mine has two young children and a full-time job. That's enough to keep anyone busy, but he has been going to night school for two years to earn his law degree. He and his wife place a high value on education and personal growth. If they didn't, they'd never be willing to sacrifice as much as they have to pursue the degree.

We need to clarify our values because our goals will arise from them. And if we don't keep our values in mind, the myriad demands on our time will tend to crowd out the things that are most essential. I have another friend who still gets tears in his eyes every time he tells me about his regrets in neglecting his family. His value system said that family was the most vital thing in his life, yet he allowed his career to keep him away from home most of the time while his children were growing up. That time can never be made up. It's a too-familiar story.

Action   List your top five values. Making this list will be a prelude to the next step, identifying your goals.

What things do you hold most dear in life? They might include the following:

- Having a good relationship with God

- Having a solid relationship with your spouse

- Investing in children

- Achieving personal growth

- Developing your gifts

- Attaining financial security

- Cultivating friendships

- Participating in church-related activities

- Giving

- Serving others

- Keeping a simple life

Developing a separate list for work can also be useful. When I made a list for my role as vice president of World Vision, it included caring for each employee, creating an entrepreneurial environment where ideas are freely exchanged, and having a service orientation toward our donors. I posted a list of my five top values near my desk. It reminded me each day to focus on what was most important.

13 ■■ Set Clear Goals

> *Most people vastly overestimate what they can accomplish in a day and vastly underestimate what they can accomplish in five years.*
> —Ted W. Engstrom

Background Most of us are reluctant to set goals. We think, *If I set a goal, it seems that I'm setting myself up to fail. I'm putting pressure on myself, and there's a good chance I'll be disappointed.*

I thought that way until a few years ago. I had so many things going on in my life that I finally faced the fact I couldn't do all of them. I was trying to write three books, consult with two companies, and continue my full-time job. I knew I had to prioritize.

I started by reflecting on my values. I then sorted through all my projects and set three simple goals for the rest of that year. I was amazed at the sense of clarity the exercise gave me. I've been hooked on setting goals ever since.

Goals help us say no. When our goals are clear, we avoid the tendency to take on more than we can actually do. We also can avoid the many distractions in our lives—the little things that seem important at the moment but really have little value, such as reading the newspaper. And people get far more done when they focus on completing just a few things rather than run from task to task with priorities constantly reshuffling.

Action Set three goals for yourself for the next two years. If you could accomplish only three things in the next two years, what would they be?

Now back up and set three goals for the next ninety days. What three things can you do in the next ninety days to make significant progress toward your two-year goals?

With these ninety-day goals in mind, what three things should you do this week?

With a little practice, you'll find that you can use this simple goal-setting exercise for all the areas of your life. I have goals for my personal life, my professional life, my weight, my finances, and so on.

I have learned that the best times for me to set goals are the beginning of the new year and my birthday. These are times when I naturally look forward. I review my goals about once a month.

Don't be afraid to fall short of your goals. My experience is that I achieve about two-thirds of my goals. Some goals will change due to circumstances; some will change because you changed your mind. That's all right. Goals are not to be shackles but to be tools to bring focus to your life today. Be flexible with them.

14 ■ Learn to Say No

We are much more apt to ask, "How can we do it?" than "What's worthwhile doing?"

—Sam Keen

Background *No* is one of the hardest words I know to say. Those of us who love people and want to be loved are reluctant to turn others down. There have been many times when I felt I should stay home to be with my family. Instead, I've found myself agreeing to do something someone asked me to do.

Saying no is much easier if you have clear goals. If you know you have a problem with taking on too much, and you haven't set clear goals, go back to the last chapter, and do yourself a big favor by setting them.

I've been helped by realizing that even Jesus couldn't do everything. He came to one small corner of the world, and on a given day He touched only a few people. Even then He often withdrew to the mountains to be alone. He knew He needed times of prayer and rest. He had a core group of twelve disciples because He knew He couldn't invest Himself adequately in more. Among the Twelve, three were his closest friends, and one was called "the disciple whom Jesus loved."

If Jesus knew His limitations, surely we can admit that we have some, too.

Action Practice saying no. If something arises that is not consistent with your current goals, refuse to get involved. Nothing saves time faster than refusing to get involved in the first place. If it is pressing, and you feel perhaps you should do it, revise your goals and drop something else.

Protect time to be with your family. It's perfectly legitimate to tell someone, "I'm sorry, but we already have plans that night." Your plans could be to stay home as a family.

Say no to the phone. Tricia and I will not interrupt a nice dinner to answer the phone. We have an answering machine, and if a friend calls, we'll return the call later that night. The phone does not give others the right to interrupt you at their convenience!

15 ■ Plan Ahead

Diligence is the mother of good fortune.
—Miguel de Cervantes

Background A wealthy industrialist once asked a management consultant to follow him through the day and advise him on how to be more effective. At the end of the day, the consultant presented a simple idea: "Before you go home each night, make a list of what you hope to get done the next day. Then prioritize the list. When you come in the next day, start working on number one. Don't go on to number two until number one is done. Do the same with each item." The industrialist asked for the consultant's bill, but the consultant told him to try the idea for two weeks and then pay him whatever he thought it was worth. Three weeks later, the consultant received a check for $25,000, a huge sum in those days.

Action This is one of the simplest and most effective time management techniques ever invented. If you follow it, you'll never fall behind on the things that really matter.

Late each day, list the priorities for the next day. Part of the genius in this idea is that your perspective on the next day is clear and unhurried at the end of the previous day.

Cultivate Your Spirit

You are a three-part creature—body, soul, and
spirit. The spirit has been greatly neglected in
modern life.

16 ■ Practice Awareness of God

> *The time of business does not with me differ from the time of prayer; and in the noise and clatter of my kitchen, while several persons are at the same time calling for different things, I possess God in as great tranquillity as if I were upon my knees at the blessed sacrament.*
> —Brother Lawrence

Background This monk, Brother Lawrence, has inspired millions to cultivate an awareness of God since he wrote his seventeenth-century classic book *The Practice of the Presence of God.* His one point is that anyone can sense God's presence virtually all the time.

God is always here. We forget Him, not the other way around. We can learn to remember Him throughout our day, and this awareness will bring clarity, peace, and simplicity to our lives.

Action The practice of awareness of God's presence is simple. Seek to remember Him as often as possible. Allow things in your life to remind you of Him—the beauty of flowers and trees, the song of a bird, whatever works.

Whenever you remember God, pray silently, thanking Him that He is still with you, asking Him to guide you, asking Him to keep reminding you that He is with you.

Practicing awareness of God doesn't happen easily. Many people have worked at it for weeks or months and still feel they are only just beginning. If you get discouraged, remember that even the desire is a sign that you're well on your way.

17 ■ Turn Off the Adrenaline

*Don't hurry, don't worry. You're only here
for a short visit.*
—Walter C. Hagen

Background   Our bodies give us one very simple and accurate clue to whether we are living peacefully—it's adrenaline. Adrenaline production was intended as a survival mechanism. For short periods of time, it allows the body to perform far beyond normal capabilities. It boosts heart rate, dilates blood vessels, heightens awareness, pulls blood away from the extremities toward vital organs, increases muscular strength, and deadens pain.

Due to the effects of adrenaline, human beings have lifted cars to free persons pinned underneath; soldiers have run or dragged themselves when their wounds were nearly fatal. And athletes perform at their peak ability by psyching themselves into producing adrenaline.

There's a dark side to adrenaline. The body pays a price for it. People have performed superhuman feats, completely unaware that they were tearing muscles in the process. But an even bigger problem is that many of us are pumping adrenaline through our systems nearly every day. The body was not intended to endure so much.

Some doctors now believe that adrenaline may be the link between Type A behavior and heart

disease. Type A behavior is largely a modern phe-
nomenon. Persons with Type A behavior are
driven to accomplishments. They find it difficult to
rest or to wait. They are always hurrying. I believe
we are not born this way; our modern culture
works with our own anxieties and produces adrenaline.

Many of us are often aware of our cold hands—
the surest sign of adrenaline flowing. Others develop headaches, tightness in the neck and shoulders, or perspiration.

We must turn off the adrenaline. It's appropriate
when we are truly in a fight-or-flight situation (for
example, facing a mugger), when we are working
toward a peak performance (for example, preparing for a public speech or an athletic event), or
when an emergency calls for all our strength. It's
not appropriate when we are driving in traffic, discussing a pet project with a colleague, or interacting with our families.

Action   The first step is to become aware of
adrenaline. The cold hands are the easiest sign to
spot. Begin to be aware when adrenaline starts to
surge through your system.

The second step is to be reflective immediately.
When you're aware of adrenaline, ask yourself, Is
it appropriate? Do I need the adrenaline to handle
this situation, or am I overreacting?

The third step is to take positive steps to cool
down. I have learned that if I am upset in traffic
and developing that familiar urge to dart around

the slow cars, I should pick one lane and stay in it. If I'm getting off the freeway in a few miles, I'll stay in the right lane. If I'm going a long way, I'll pick one of the middle lanes and stay there. Once I make the decision, it's surprising how quickly I calm down.

Stopping the adrenaline will take practice. If I'm upset in a business meeting, I may not have the opportunity to excuse myself and take a leisurely walk to the water cooler. But I can at least be aware of my adrenaline and try my best to keep perspective on the meeting. Rarely is it a matter of life-and-death consequences.

When you're not able to avoid a burst of adrenaline, you should schedule time to recover. Your body was not meant to sustain that pace, and you need to give it a break. After a speech, I'll try to leave time to sleep late the next morning. After a tough morning of meetings, I'll have lunch by myself. The most critical issue is to not allow the fast pace to carry on any longer than necessary. As soon as possible, slow down.

18 ■ Advance with a Retreat

I love to be alone. I never found the companion that was so companionable as solitude.

—Henry David Thoreau

Background When we think of taking a retreat, we usually don't think of the literal meaning of the word: to move backward. In reality, taking a personal retreat is a big move forward. Perhaps we should call it an advance.

Have you ever taken one whole day just to be alone? I'd never done such a thing until a few years ago. I had to be in another town, and I had most of the day alone. At the time, I didn't like being alone. It made me nervous. I felt lonely.

For some reason, at that particular time of my life, I felt I had some personal work to do. I was dissatisfied and didn't know why. I knew I'd never figure it out until I could spend time alone.

I took a notebook and began by working through the high points of the last few years: What was I most happy with? Then I worked through the low points: What would I like to change? When I began feeling restless, I'd change scenery—go to a mall or drive to the beach. For seven or eight hours, I wrestled with myself. Some of the most fundamental directions in my life today are the result of that time. I resolved to get in shape. I resolved to explore the effects of my troubled childhood with a counselor. I resolved to show more love to my wife and to give work a smaller place in my heart so there would be more room for her.

Since that time, I've tried to repeat this experience at least twice a year.

Action   Schedule time to take a retreat. If you're a businessperson, perhaps you can take an earlier flight when you have to travel and use the time in another city. If you're a parent, hire a baby-sitter and find a quiet place in the library or at a park.

Many churches will help with retreats. The older traditions—Catholic, Lutheran, Episcopalian—tend to actively promote this idea for their members. They often have their own retreat centers, which are usually available to anyone.

Start your retreat with prayer. Prayer opens your spirit to God's influence. If you aren't practiced with prayer, don't worry. It's the heart that matters, not the eloquence.

Reflect on the past. Where have you fallen short? What are you most happy with?

Consider the future. What would you like to change? Be sure to write—the more, the better. You will be surprised at the passion that flows, and if you don't write it down, you'll forget important elements of your thought process.

Close your retreat with prayer. Offer your plans and dreams to God, and ask Him to give you the strength to carry out your good intentions.

Make Peace with Your Enemies

Life is too short to spend it in hate. Hate consumes the hater more than the hated.

19 ∷ Forgive

To err is human, to forgive divine.
—Alexander Pope

Background Unforgiveness can ruin your life. When someone slights you, offends you, or deeply hurts you, the urge to respond in kind is a natural reaction: an eye for an eye, a tooth for a tooth. But giving in to that urge takes its toll not only on the offender; it can consume the one seeking revenge.

In biblical times, Jewish law allowed for such revenge. Whatever someone did to you, you were allowed to do to that person. If you were killed, your relatives could take the life of your killer. To prevent hasty "justice" when someone may have been killed by accident, the law established cities of refuge. If you killed someone accidentally, you could flee to a city of refuge, and as long as you remained within that city, no one could touch you. If you ever ventured outside the city, you could be killed. Some relatives would wait for years to catch a man outside the city and kill him in revenge.

The Hatfields and the McCoys were real people. Their feud entered into legend and stretched across several generations. Today, various ethnic groups in the Middle East, Catholics and Protestants in Northern Ireland, and gangs in East Los Angeles perpetuate revenge that is out of control.

Far more common are the little things that we

let separate us from family members and friends. Someone said something and we let it fester for years. An argument that developed on one of our bad days blew up into a lifelong break with a brother. A friend lets us down and we stop investing in that friendship.

Action   The nature of human beings is such that we grate on one another at times. It happens in the best of relationships. We must learn to forgive. Forgiveness means that I choose to let you be imperfect. I accept you even though you may have hurt me.

Being forgiving doesn't mean just rolling over and accepting the situation. If someone offends you, you should go to that person and say what's bothering you. The hurt gets out into the open where it can be dealt with. If the person refuses to apologize, you should ask someone else to be an arbitrator. The third party can help you and the person be fair to each other.

Ultimately, if the person apologizes, you have no choice but to forgive. If the person won't apologize, you have a tough choice. Will you let this situation separate you permanently from the other person, or will you find it in yourself to forgive anyway? Unless the offense really does deserve to separate the two of you (for example, repeated unfaithfulness of a spouse), you will be far better off if you can find the strength to forgive.

Sometimes people hurt you deeply, especially if it's someone you love very much. Offering forgiveness doesn't mean the pain will stop. Rather, each time the pain comes back, you look beyond it. I like to think in terms of driving on a dark road at night. When the oncoming headlights are in your eyes, you can steer by the white line at the side of the road. When the hurt returns, you remember that you have made a choice to forgive, and you do your best to look away from the hurt and to continue moving forward.

20 ■ Channel Your Anger

Anger is the emotion that tells us our boundaries are being violated.
—John Bradshaw

Background   Having enemies takes enormous energy. When I have an enemy, I must stay on guard. I must watch my flank lest my enemy take advantage of me. I imagine all sorts of conversations with my enemy—how I'd like to tell him a thing or two! These imaginary conversations can consume all my waking thoughts.

I have had to work diligently at dealing with enemies in my life. It's hard for me to confront another person when I feel my rights are violated. I'd rather suffer in silence, just suck it in.

I saw a cartoon recently that made me laugh out loud. It showed a series of caves with cavemen standing out front. All the cavemen were looking in the direction of one particular cave. In front of that cave was a portly caveman; he was sloppily dressed and surrounded by mastodon bones and carcasses. The caption read, "There's one in every neighborhood."

We lived in a neighborhood that had its own version of this caveman—the guy with a boat, an RV, and four cars. His vehicles lined the street in front of my house for months. I'd smile at the man, but inwardly, I was seething. I began to imagine that he left the vehicles there to make me mad. I pictured going down to his house to ask him to move the vehicles, but in my imagination he always said something nasty, which would cause me to respond in kind. I decided a confrontation wasn't worth it, and I tried to ignore the situation.

Finally, the day came when we put our house up for sale. Our agent suggested that we should clear the street in front of our house, or its value might be diminished. I was forced to act. I gritted my teeth, marched down to the neighbor, and steeled myself for the scene to come. What happened was what I had least expected. My neighbor said he'd be glad to move them, and they were never again in front of my house.

The point is, not until we take positive steps to resolve anger will we be able to have peace.

Forgiving my neighbor in advance would have softened my anger. I could have asked him to move his vehicles without fear of exploding at him. I could have decided that if he wouldn't move them, it wouldn't mean he was an awful person. If I had to, I could live with the situation. I'd rather look at the vehicles than hate a neighbor.

At our next house, we found we could see a neighbor's old boat until the trees leaved out in the spring. Soon after meeting him, I asked my neighbor if he'd move the boat in the fall. He agreed without hesitation.

Anger is actually a healthy emotion. It creates problems when we don't act appropriately on it.

Make Peace with Your Enemies

Action When you feel anger, act on it that very day. If you do, there's much less chance of its getting out of control. Repressed anger will someday burst forth like a volcano.

Tricia and I have a compact that if we are even slightly offended by each other, we will bring it up the same day. If I cut her off while talking to friends, she'll let me know later that night that I hurt her feelings. Before our agreement, I would have found out about the offense months later, after I'd done it a dozen times. By then, it would have come out in an explosion, "You always cut me off, and I'm sick of it . . ." I would then, of course, respond defensively. Now, we rarely have angry arguments. We are able to deal with the normal tensions of married life productively.

Resolve to act quickly and positively when you feel anger, before it grows into something out of proportion to the problem. Don't become a Hatfield or a McCoy.

21 ▪ Seek Help for Difficult Relationships

Fifty percent of married couples will probably never be happy unless they get genuine professional help.
—David Olson, University of Minnesota researcher, from a study of 15,300 couples

Background Sometimes a relationship is just not working. You seem to be spiraling downward. If the relationship is important, it's worth seeking help. These days many professionals can help you work through relationship problems. And many of these problems stem from past experiences, often in your childhood. Trying to work through them on your own is not nearly as effective as gaining insights from an unbiased, well-qualified outsider.

I've seen many marriages, including my own, where the two people are driven by needs they don't understand, needs arising from childhood. The needs of one can feed right into the needs of the other and create a seemingly impossible situation.

I have two friends, a man and a woman, who seem made for each other. All their friends want them to get married. But they have been on-again, off-again for six years now. He has a fear of abandonment, stretching back to his childhood. He needs a woman who will be committed to him. Because she has been unable to make this commitment, he is now paralyzed by fear, an irrational fear that, even if they marry, she will ultimately leave him.

She, in turn, has a fear of conditional love since she never felt that she was intrinsically worthy of love. Love was always given to her based on her performance. She needs a man who will not pressure her to get married because she feels she is loved only as long as she performs. Pressure to marry feels to her like conditional love. They are seeking professional help, and the outcome is not yet clear. But at least they are doing something positive about the difficult relationship.

Action   If you are having serious difficulties in a close relationship, life will not seem simple until you deal with the root problems. No matter what else you do to simplify your life, the relationship will weigh on you. Seek help.

There are lots of alternatives these days: marriage and family counselors, psychologists, and psychiatrists. These professionals specialize in relational problems and must undergo certification in most states, assuring that they've had proper education and internship.

Many churches offer free counseling by a pastor trained in counseling.

One word of caution is in order: Be sure the counselor shares your values. You'll want to determine this at the beginning. I've heard sad tales of counselors who drove wedges in marriages by their biases. One woman I know was advised to leave her husband because "women are better off alone, free of the restrictions of a marriage." I know another woman whose counselor made inappropriate sexual comments to her. Fortunately, she saw this early and got out before she became vulnerable.

Simplify Your Finances

Control your money; don't let it control you.

22 ■■ Use a Budget

Instead of studying how to make it worth men's while to buy my baskets, I studied rather how to avoid the necessity of selling them.

—Henry David Thoreau

Background Thoreau's wisdom on this point is profound and rarely followed. For all the energy we put into trying to get more money, we might put just a little into reducing our need for money instead!

You cannot have simplicity in your finances without a budget. You cannot have control over your money unless you know where it's going and make decisions about it *in advance.* Unfortunately, thousands of individuals and companies out there want your money. And they aren't shy about going after it. Marketers study what makes you tick and how to get you to part with your money for things you don't really need.

A major marketing study a few years ago discovered that the deepest felt need for men in America was companionship. For women, the deepest need was to be cherished. Notice the most common theme in commercials? For products aimed at men, it's a group of buddies having fun together. For products aimed at women, it's being caressed because your skin is so soft or kissed because your mouth is so fresh and so on.

There are a thousand other tricks in the marketer's hat. Believe me; I've been one for over ten years. Studies have been done on everything from the layout of the store to the type of music played —all designed to make you spend more money.

The only way you can navigate the treacherous waters of the Buy Me Sea and safely reach the other side is to make wise decisions about money away from the point of purchase. That's exactly what a budget does. You make your decisions in advance, and you track your expenses against those decisions, making course corrections as necessary.

Action   If you've never done a budget, don't be intimidated. A budget doesn't have to be so restrictive that it takes all the fun out of life. Tricia and I have found it to be freeing. We even give ourselves an allowance—a little money each month that we can spend however we desire.

To prepare a budget, do the best you can to reconstruct where your money went last month. Take your checkbook, pay stubs, and charge account statements, and combine expenses into ten or fifteen categories—for example, auto, clothing, food, housing, and entertainment. If you pay many of your expenses in cash, you may not be able to reconstruct all of last month. You may need to keep track for a month or two. If it's too tedious to write down every expense for a month, note how much cash you have available for each day and endeavor at the end of the day to identify where it went.

When you have some history, develop a rough

plan for where you want to spend your money this month. Track it as closely as you can, and evaluate at the end of the month how well you did. With some experience, you'll find you are making changes. You'll decide to cut back a little in one area to avoid going into debt or to save for a major purchase.

The hardest part of budgeting is that you may find that you are spending more than you are making. Although that's a rude awakening, it's better to know it now than to figure it out when you're nearly bankrupt!

If you have a computer, several programs are available (for example, Quicken and Managing Your Money) that will reduce the amount of time it takes to pay bills and balance the checkbook. And they automatically keep track of actual expenses versus a budget. Using a computerized approach has been a great help to Tricia and me. We take at most a half hour each month to review the report that Quicken prints out for us and discuss changes to the budget for the next month.

23 ■ Pay Off Your Mortgage Early

Thirty-year mortgages make mortgage companies rich.

—Charles J. Givens

Background If you borrowed $100,000 at 10 percent interest for thirty years, after ten years of making payments you would have paid the mortgage company $105,000—more than you originally owed—and you would still owe $91,000. That is not a misprint. The fact is, when you spread payments over thirty years, you are paying virtually nothing toward the principal on your loan until the last ten years. And if you ever reach that glorious day when you have made the last payment, be aware that you have paid a total of $316,000—more than three times what you borrowed.

If you added only $200 per month to your payment to be used against principal, you would have paid $129,000 in ten years, but you would owe only $50,000. Your mortgage would be paid off in fifteen years, at a total cost of $193,000. By adding only $200 per month, you save $123,000 in interest. And what will you do with all the money you have for the next fifteen years, free of mortgage payments?

Less than 2 percent of Americans own their homes free and clear. The majority of retirees still carry a mortgage that has more years remaining than their projected life span. By paying only $200 more a month (or proportionally more if you owe more than $100,000), you can own your home in fifteen years and save $100,000 or more in interest.

Action Start this month. Find the money somewhere. Pay an extra $200 per month toward your mortgage, and determine to own your home while you're still young enough to enjoy the freedom. Can you imagine how much you will simplify your life when you no longer have a mortgage payment? Keep asking yourself that question and you will soon not miss the $200.

The only qualification to this advice is that some mortgages contain a prepayment penalty. They are rare these days, but ask your lender to be sure that your loan agreement allows you to prepay toward the principal.

24 ■ Fast from Buying

I see young men, my townsmen, whose misfortune it is to have inherited farms, houses, barns, cattle, and farming tools; for these are more easily acquired than got rid of.

—Henry David Thoreau

Background We all have our soft spots. For me, it tends to be books. For my wife, it's clothes. Both of us have a weakness for going out to eat.

It's important that we break these spending habits from time to time, especially if we have a tendency to buy things to lift our spirits when we're feeling blue, or if we tend to buy on impulse.

A fast from buying is simply a decision that I won't buy something for a specified period of time. I might decide that I have enough unread books to last awhile. No matter how many great books I see, I will not buy another one until I finish the ones I have. Tricia will occasionally decide not to buy any clothes for a few months. We may decide not to eat out this month because we are adjusting our budget to save for a large purchase.

Far from stifling, these fasts are freeing. One decision can save dozens of smaller ones. I can learn to be more detached from what I own. I can focus on lifting my spirits by enjoying nature or seeking a closer relationship with God rather than making a trip to the mall.

Action If anything is getting the best of your budget, decide to go on a fast. Determine that no matter what happens, you will not spend money on that particular item for a specified period of time. It's much easier to accumulate useless things than it is to live wisely. To live simply in our consumer culture, we must live above the seduction that is constantly trying to get us to define ourselves by what we own. We must not buy what we do not need. If we hope to live up to that commitment, we must occasionally fast from buying even good things. It's good for building discipline.

25 ■ Save 10 Percent for Yourself

And you shall spend that money for whatever your heart desires: for oxen or sheep, for wine or similar drink, for whatever your heart desires; you shall eat there before the LORD your God, and you shall rejoice, you and your household.
—Deuteronomy 14:26

Background Who says God is no fun? God set a practice here that amounts to a giant party.

Life has enough trials without constant financial worries. As I have progressed in my business career, I have learned one certain truth: I'll never have *enough* money. No matter how big the raises, they always disappear into my budget.

The only solution to this dilemma is to budget ourselves to live on 90 percent of our income. Personally, I try to make do with 80 percent, so I can give away 10 percent and save another 10 percent.

If you can save 10 percent of your income, it's amazing what happens to your attitude. There's always a cushion. There's no more fear when the car breaks down, the tax bill is higher than expected, or an appliance needs to be replaced. Charles J. Givens, in his book *Wealth Without Risk,* suggests you save at this level for two years until you have 20 percent of your annual income in savings. He calls it "attitude money."

Action It's not pleasant to think of saving money for two years just to have a cushion, but it's one of the soundest pieces of advice I've seen. Develop a budget and work toward saving 10 percent each month. In chapter 31, "Invest Simply," I'll tell you what to do with the money.

After you've saved two years' worth—when you have 20 percent of your annual income in savings —start spending that 10 percent each year on whatever your heart desires, as the Bible suggests. Life will seem a lot more pleasant.

26 ▪ Have Fun Saving Money

*I like ironing your shirts now that I get
paid for it!*

—My wife, Tricia

Background No one likes to save money,
right? Wrong. You can make saving money fun.
The secret is to come up with creative ways to
reward yourself for saving.

Tricia has always hated ironing, so I've done my
own shirts. When I began traveling frequently, I no
longer had the time. I decided to start taking my
shirts to the cleaners. Then I had an idea. If Tricia
ironed any of my shirts, I'd give her the same
amount of money that I'd pay the cleaners. It
would be "above-budget" money. In other words, if
she had spent the budgeted amount for clothes
already, she could use this extra money she
earned from ironing. Much to my surprise, she began to enjoy ironing! She also saves coupons now
—something she had never wanted to do. She
keeps track of how much she saves, and she uses
the money for whatever she wants. We already
give ourselves a monthly allowance to spend on
whatever we wish. This extra money is over and
above that.

A friend takes his wife to Florida every year on

what they save using coupons. Another friend goes to Europe on the money he and his wife save from having only one car. He takes the train to work every day—an inconvenience, certainly—but the payoff is worth it. They love their yearly vacation in Europe.

Action   Think of ways you could save money, but you haven't been motivated enough to do it— clipping coupons, taking your lunch to work, making do with one car, taking a cheaper flight, and so on. Then think of a way to reward the family member who made the sacrifice, or decide to share the reward—have a night out for dinner, a vacation, or something that the whole family will enjoy.

27 ■■ Avoid Debt

Debt is the worst poverty.
—M. G. Lightner

Background Debt is one sure way to complicate life. The more debt you have, the less control
you have over your finances, and the more your
energy and thoughts will be consumed with
money. You have to work harder just to stay even.

We live in a society that encourages debt for virtually any expense. Only a few decades ago, even
home mortgages were given for ten years or less,
and it was impossible to get loans for cars. These
days people use charge cards for virtually anything, even groceries.

Action Avoid debt. Don't borrow to buy anything unless you could resell what you bought and
pay off the loan (such as a house or a stable investment). Even for a house, use the strategy discussed in chapter 24 to pay off the mortgage in
fifteen years, saving $100,000 or more in interest.

If you cannot discipline yourself to pay off your
charge cards every month, cut them up. Never go
into debt for things like clothes, vacations, or
stereo equipment. If you have trouble paying the
money back, you have nothing to sell. You are a
slave to that debt.

Buying a new car on credit is poor stewardship

of your resources. If you borrow money to buy a new car, it will be two years before you owe less than what the car is worth. In other words, if you have to sell the car, you will need to come up with extra money to pay off the loan. Let others take this huge loss. If you need a car, buy one that's two years old. It's still relatively new, but it's past the time when a car's value drops rapidly.

Most banks will loan on two-year-old cars at close to the same interest rate as new cars. (They know that a two-year-old car is a good value!)

28 ■■ Ignore Fads and Fashions

Hang the fashions. Buy only what you need.

—Richard Foster

Background   Fashions are an incredible waste of money. A coat is discarded because it's out-of-date, even though it still performs its function perfectly well. A closet is full of ties too wide or too narrow. Practically new pants are the "wrong" color.

Fashions are created by the clothing industry. Some smart person long ago figured out that fashion trends could induce people to buy far more clothes than they really need.

You don't have to give in to this pressure.

Action   Refuse to buy trendy clothes. You know when something is likely to be a short-lived fashion.

Men can avoid the problem with suits and ties by loading up when the lapel and tie widths are somewhere in the middle. Don't buy when they're at their widest or narrowest. If you really feel you need to look up-to-date, buy just one of the latest wild ties. Resist the temptation to look trendy every day.

It's a little more difficult for women, but there are skirt lengths and classic cuts that never go out of style.

Abiding by this suggestion is more difficult with children. Their self-images are fragile, and the peer pressure is intense. Don't be so strict that they suffer constant embarrassment, but do set limits. Some of the trends, such as superexpensive tennis shoes, are ridiculous.

For every season and every occasion, there are some clothes that are always in style. Fill most of your wardrobe with them, and wear them until they're worn out.

Keep your children away from TV, and they won't be clamoring for the latest toy. I think it's a crime to let children spend endless hours playing with electronic gadgets when there's a whole world for them to experience and explore. Buy them toys that stretch their minds, for example, telescopes or microscopes; better yet, take them out into the great outdoors, and teach them about the local plants and animals.

If we could escape from the bombardment of advertising, we'd soon realize we need very little to live a full life. Unfortunately, we can't get away from it, but we can fight against the temptation to have the latest, greatest new thing.

29 ■ Don't Compete with the Joneses

There are two ways to get enough: one is to continue to accumulate more and more. The other is to desire less.
—G. K. Chesterton

Background Keeping up with the Joneses is an age-old game. If we don't look as prosperous as the folks next door, how can we hold our heads high in the neighborhood? There's no end to this game—and no winner.

Action Impress people with your life, not with your things. And don't let your children use their friends as the standard for what they need. Teach them while they're young that the only standard we live by is what is right for us. We develop our standards by being sensitive to God and neighbor but never by trying to keep up with the neighbor.

Buy items such as cars and clothes for function, not for the potential to impress others.

30 ■■ Invest Simply

There are two times in a man's life when he should not speculate: when he can't afford it, and when he can.

—Mark Twain

Background Investments can complicate our lives in one of two ways. First, we can be so driven to get the highest return possible that we take unwise risks and end up losing money. Almost everyone I know has lost some money this way. Fortunately, it's been a lesson we've learned before we had much money to invest. There's an old adage among investment professionals that says, "If it sounds too good to be true, it is."

The other way is to let investments worry us. If we are worrying about our money, we may as well give it away. Life is too short to spend it worrying about money. I've never seen a rich person I thought was happy because of the money. And I've seen Ethiopians with nothing who were joyful and happy.

I'm not going to say, "Get rid of your money." For most of us, investments are necessary—to provide for our children's education and our old age if nothing else.

Simple investments are within our reach. Simple investments have a track record of reasonable returns through all types of economic ups and downs. They are secure—they can't be easily stolen or evaporate when a risky deal goes sour.

And they are places we can leave our money without needing to make decisions week by week or even month by month.

Action   One simple investment is the stock market—but not individual stocks. You should never buy individual stocks unless you are a professional. Forget all the hot tips; all the decks are stacked against the individual investor. If your Uncle Harry knows something about a company, the pros knew it long ago, and it's already reflected in the price. That is, unless Uncle Harry works for the company and is giving you inside information. In that case, you and Harry can go to jail if you profit from it.

Stock mutual funds are probably the best long-term investment for individuals. They return approximately 12 percent per year over the long haul. They are, however, subject to many ups and downs along the way, and you should not invest money in stock mutual funds that you may need to pull out on short notice. You should also not invest a lump sum all at once. The market may go down next week and you are suddenly behind. Do what the pros call dollar cost-averaging. Invest a little at a time, every week or every month. Over time, your price per share will average out, and you stand a better chance of making a good return.

Money market funds provide a safe alternative for money that you may need soon. They return less than stocks, but they are much less subject to fluctuation. They usually allow you to write checks against your account.

Rental houses have also tended to be a good investment for the average individual investor. The main problem with rental houses is that you have the headaches of maintaining the homes, dealing with tenants, advertising, and so on. The tax laws are hard to keep up with, too. I don't think rental houses will simplify your life, but if you have time —if you are retired, for example—they can be good investments.

Invest simply, and give up trying to make a killing.

31 ■ Give It Away

As the purse is emptied, the heart is filled.
—Victor Hugo

Background Are you tired of money controlling you? Jacques Ellul, in his book *Money and Power,* uses Jesus' teachings about money to make the case that money is a rival god. It tends to take over your life. You serve and worship it without even realizing it. He prescribes the way to break that rival god's hold on your life: when you give money away, you profane it. You step outside its rules, which include: hoard and you'll have more, have more and you'll be happier, and so on. When you give, you prove to yourself again and again that money is not the root of happiness.

Your money will always have an unnatural hold on you until you learn to give. No matter what your financial status, there are always others worse off. If you earn the median income in the United States, you are included in the top 5 percent of the wealthiest people who have ever lived. Believe me, I've been all over the world, and we have it far better than we care to admit.

I believe as citizens of one globe we owe it to help others, especially the poor in other countries. I don't know how to bring equity to the situation, but as World Vision's founder Bob Pierce said,

"Just because you can't do everything doesn't mean you can't do something."

As a Christian, I believe my giving should be significant. It's not enough to give only a few dollars here and there. I use the guideline that God gave to the Jewish people in the Old Testament, 10 percent. Tricia and I give away at least 10 percent of our gross income each month, as though it were another bill to pay. That's the minimum. We try to see how far we can exceed that level. We consider it an obligation as children of God and citizens of a needy world.

Action Begin this month to give. If your budget is tight, give what you can. But change your budget so you can give more.

Find one or two charities that focus on causes you care deeply about. Read their literature. Become informed about the causes. Request the charities' annual reports, and pay close attention to the percentage spent on fund-raising and administration. Anything over 25 or 30 percent is unreasonable.

Most charities are listed with the Better Business Bureau (BBB). If the charity is not approved by the BBB, find another one.

Don't just give to causes far away; give locally, too. If you go to church, give to the church. If you are benefiting from the pastor and the programs, contribute to their support.

You will be especially rewarded if you can give to something locally and see the rewards of your giving. Visit a local shelter or soup kitchen and watch your gifts at work.

I also believe in direct giving to the homeless in my community. They are reminders of how blessed I am. I don't want to always cross the street to avoid them. I want to say some kind words, learn more about their situation, and do what I can to help. That will keep me from being cold and cut off from others' suffering. I know they might use the money I give them to drink. I make them promise they won't, and if I don't believe them, I don't give. But ultimately, my reward is in the giving. What they do with the money is their responsibility.

Don't just give money; give clothes, furniture, and other items you no longer need. Many worthy charities survive primarily through these donations. Go through your closets once a year. If you haven't worn something in a year, you don't need it. Give it to someone who does.

Do It Yourself

You should do some things for yourself. Miss
them, and you'll miss a blessing.

32 ■ Enjoy Manual Labor

*The whole long day of hard work had left
on them no trace of anything but merri-
ment.*

—Leo Tolstoy

Background Any weekend gardener can testify to what Tolstoy, Thoreau, and others have said:
manual labor is good for us. It's invigorating. It's
healthy for our hearts, and it tones our muscles. It
allows us to lose track of time and let our minds
relax.

Manual labor is none too glorious for the coal
miner or the day laborer, but for most of us who
live sedentary lives and work primarily with our
minds, it is beneficial for us. I enjoy chopping
wood or building something. Tricia and I love to
garden, and for this labor, we're rewarded with delicious produce!

There's nothing like manual labor to wring the
stress out of my back and neck muscles. After a
week of office work, I'm ready for the peace of
some manual labor (and a long nap afterward!).

Action Find something you enjoy doing that
works your muscles and leaves your mind free to
wander. Life will make more sense after an hour or
two of manual labor. And I promise you'll sleep
better.

33 ■ Plant a Garden

Might I have a bit of earth?
—Frances Hodgson Burnett

Background If you have any space at all in your yard, a garden is one of the true joys of life. It's an outlet for occasional manual labor, yet it doesn't require too much. It saves money. The food you grow is better for you than food picked weeks earlier and shipped to the market. Most of all, the food tastes great. Home-grown corn or tomatoes are so sweet, you'll wonder if they're the same species as the store-bought varieties.

There's something almost mystical about having a garden. You put small seeds into wet earth, water them occasionally, and watch your work cooperate with God's creation.

Action This spring, plant a small garden. Find out what grows well in your climate. Ask your friends what they have grown. I personally think corn and tomatoes are the most rewarding because they come out so much tastier than the ones you buy. But so do peas, berries, and many other crops.

If you don't have much land, try growing a few things in pots. Herbs can even be grown indoors. Fresh herbs make any dish taste better than dry canned herbs.

34 ▪ Find a Hobby

All work and no play makes Jack a dull boy.

—James Howell

Background Everyone needs a creative outlet. If you are always working, life is a bore. Very few people are fortunate enough to find an enjoyable creative outlet in their work. Even if you love your job, a hobby helps you avoid having all your waking thoughts consumed with work. You will have a broader perspective if you are interested in more than one thing.

A hobby should be something you love to do. It should be something that creates what some call a flow experience—you become so absorbed that you lose track of time, feel fully engaged, and perceive a deep sense of satisfaction.

Action If you already have a hobby that fits this description, make sure you give time to it. Don't fall into the trap of believing you must always be accomplishing something. And don't allow lesser activities, such as watching TV, to crowd out your hobby.

If you don't have a hobby, try a few things that attract you. Is there something you used to do that you gave up for lack of time? Is there something you always wanted to do—paint or learn to play the piano? Try it!

For some people, the perfect hobby is something they loved as children but stopped doing. As a young child, I liked to write stories. For some reason, writing was not reinforced by my schooling. I think it's because I liked to write stories on whatever came to mind; I didn't want to be told what I had to write about. Writing lost its pleasure for me until I rediscovered it a few years ago. I may or may not ever sell a story. Actually, I've never tried. The important thing is that I love to do it. It calls out something from my inner self, and it's worth doing for the sheer pleasure of it.

If you are stumped, ask your friends about their hobbies. Join with them and see if you enjoy theirs. If you're still stumped, just start trying things: grow some flowers, draw something, collect something, build a model, but do something!

35 ■ Do Simple Repairs and Maintenance

I like work: it fascinates me. I can sit and look at it for hours.
                                                    —Jerome K. Jerome

Background I was recently on top of my house running a plumber's snake down a vent pipe to try to fix a clogged drain. I'd already tried clearing the drain from inside the house, and I'd tried to find a way to get at it under the house. Nothing had worked. I had announced to Tricia that I would try one more thing—from the roof—then I'd call a plumber. It's not that it had taken me very long; it's just that I was getting frustrated. I thought my first efforts should have worked.

In five minutes, Tricia was yelling that the drain was clear. What a great sense of satisfaction I felt! It was not rocket science, mind you, but I had correctly diagnosed the problem and found the solution—and it was something I'd never done before. Tricia was proud of me. I had saved the cost of a plumber, and I had learned something new. And it took me all of twenty minutes.

Many repairs are actually very simple—replacing a washer in a faucet, clearing a drain, replacing a toilet valve, even fixing malfunctions in small appliances. It's very gratifying to fix something yourself. You simplify your life by saving money. And you often save time by not having to call a professional.

Employees of hardware stores are generally very helpful with almost any problem. They'll tell you if you really should hire someone. Or they'll explain to you how to fix it.

Action Next time something breaks, give it ten or twenty minutes' effort before you pay someone else to fix it. You may still give up; that's okay. But see if you can learn to be a little more self-sufficient. In a few years, you may be an amateur plumber, carpenter, auto mechanic, and appliance repair person!

Don't Do It Yourself

There are times to do it yourself and times to let someone else do it. Wisdom is in knowing the difference!

36 ■ Hire Someone for Difficult Jobs

When the car falls on your leg, give up!
—My wife, Tricia

Background Some years ago, I was trying to fix the brakes on my car. I didn't really know what I was doing. A bolt was stuck. I pulled and pulled on the wrench—to no avail. I stuck a pipe on the wrench for more leverage. I was going to get that bolt out if it killed me! It nearly did. By the time I realized the car was falling off the jack, it was too late to pull my leg out. The car came down right on my outstretched leg. The story has a happy ending, though. The jack stands were almost exactly the width of my leg, and when the axle came to rest on them, the edge of the car had given me only a surface cut. My leg was not crushed.

That was a frightening lesson to me. I'm wiser now. I hire someone for the dangerous jobs and for the ones I don't know how to do.

I bought a new water heater last year. I had learned quite a lot about plumbing through making repairs. I was 90 percent sure I could install the new water heater by myself. I turned off the water supply and applied my wrench to the first coupling. It wouldn't budge. I tried everything—no luck. In the old days, I'd have spent half a day trying to get that coupling off, only to discover that the next one was frozen, too. I gave up after twenty minutes and called a plumber. I spent the day lounging with Tricia and felt every dollar I paid the plumber was worth it.

Action   This suggestion is an extension of the previous one. Try to do things yourself, but set a limit. If it isn't working after ten or twenty minutes —if you can't figure it out or it's not going your way—give up. There are times when the wisest move you can make is to hire a professional. Call it an investment in simplifying your life.

Never work with dangerous things unless you know what you are doing. Don't tinker with natural gas or electrical wiring. Don't open the back of a television set. And don't put your leg under a car while yanking on a bolt!

37 ⊞ Don't Accumulate Expensive Tools

Man is a tool-using animal.
—Thomas Carlyle

Background   I used to think that if I bought a tool, it didn't count in the cost of repair. After all, I would use that tool again and again. Unfortunately, that hasn't often been the case.

I've even used a home project to try to justify buying a tool that I thought would be nice to own. I almost bought a table saw. We needed bookshelves in our family room, and Mr. Fix It (that's me) thought he'd do it himself.

I began salivating over table saws in the hardware store while I calculated the cost of my materials. Luckily, I happened to receive a furniture catalog at the same time. I didn't realize how inexpensive wall units could be. For a little more than the cost of the materials, I could buy a beautiful wall unit that included drawers, cupboards, and other elements I'd never be able to build. "But I want a table saw!" I protested.

I was tempted to justify it without counting the cost of the table saw, but I realized that I couldn't be sure I'd ever use the saw again. I decided not to build it, and I am truly glad. I have never had another use for a table saw. The decision simplified my life greatly for the month it would have taken me to build the shelves. And we have a very nice wall unit instead of an amateur version that we'd probably want to give away by now.

Action Count the cost of the tools as though you'll never use them again. If it's a ten-dollar wrench, and it will save a sixty-dollar plumber's bill, by all means buy it. If you're thinking about buying a table saw and building bookshelves, reread my story!

38 ■ Find the Right Person to Help

A friend in need is a friend indeed.
—English proverb

Background Do you know what your friends do when faced with repairs or maintenance? Do you know what skills they have? If you know someone who is great with cars, you are lucky!

The world was a simpler place when neighbors helped one another. I'd help you build your barn, and you'd help me tend a sick horse. If we always take our needs to a national chain store, our lives are very impersonal.

Even if you need to pay for services, wouldn't it be nice if you could have a relationship with the people who provide the service, if you got to know them so well that you trusted them implicitly?

Action Try getting help from your friends first.

If that doesn't work, try finding people you can get to know. A moonlighting auto mechanic charges less than half what you'd pay the shop where he works during the day.

Even if you live in a large city, you can develop relationships with professionals who moonlight, small business owners, or even the manager of a large shop. It will simplify your life if you can develop a network of people you can turn to when you need help, people you can trust.

Help other people in areas where you have skills. You must give if you hope to receive—that's one of God's built-in designs for life.

Get Closer to Nature

A few decades ago, most people worked on farms. Although it's nice to be free of the backbreaking labor and the uncertainty of nature, most of us miss the effects of the seasons, the long periods of working alone, and the joys of harvest. Perhaps worst of all, we are alienated from the land that sustains us.

39 ⊞ Recycle

Let us never forget that the cultivation of the earth is the most important labor of man.

—Daniel Webster

Background The move to save the earth is a vital development. I needn't rehearse the alarming statistics related to ozone depletion, pollution, and garbage.

Recycling is a simple contribution every household can make to this cause. It doesn't take much effort. Many disposal companies now provide a separate bin for recyclable items. It's a shame if you have this service available and don't use it. For others, it's a little more trouble but worthwhile nevertheless. We in the U.S. have 6 percent of the world's population and use 35 percent of the world's resources. How long do you think that can last? And ask yourself, Is it fair?

Action Start this week to recycle. Separate the recyclable cans and bottles from your trash. If you aren't sure where to take them, just keep your eyes open. You probably drive past a recycling center every day. Or the local newspaper may list recycling sites and hours.

Watch for school newspaper drives. Giving your newspapers to them is a good way to recycle and help a worthy cause at the same time.

If you have a garden, start a compost pile. Fertilizer takes enormous energy, and the runoff pollutes streams and rivers. Composting is really quite simple.

You'll start feeling like a responsible world citizen when you realize that half your garbage is going to some good use.

40 ▪▪ Buy with Sensitivity to the Rest of the World

Are we as willing to evaluate our living standards by the needs of the poor as we are by the lifestyle of our neighbors?
—Richard Foster

Background Most of us don't think about how our consumption affects anything else but us. But occasionally, the harmful effects become the center of attention. One example is the use of pesticide and its effects on farm workers. Another is the issue of trade with South Africa.

We should think about the effects we have on the poor, but we should also think about animals and the environment. One issue that represents a success story is the destruction of dolphins to catch tuna. It took a little time for the tuna companies to switch to dolphin-safe methods. They were unwilling to change their methods until the public caught on. They finally decided that there were enough of us who cared. The tuna companies would not have changed their ways by themselves. There had to be enough people who would be willing to pay more for tuna caught by methods that didn't hurt dolphins. Thankfully, there were.

Action Be a person who cares, and translate that caring into your buying decisions.

Buy products that don't have wasteful packaging. If the packaging is twice as large as it needs to be, look for another brand.

Avoid non-recyclable plastic and Styrofoam whenever possible. Every non-recyclable plastic bottle and Styrofoam cup you've ever used will still be sitting in the ground centuries after you're gone.

Look for the recycle insignia, and buy products made from recycled materials.

Be aware of the human cost of products. Avoid products from companies whose workers are mistreated.

Every small action adds up. An Ethiopian proverb says, "If enough spiders unite, they can tie up a lion." Never give in to the defeatist attitude that you can't make a difference.

41 ◫ Get Outside

For many years I was self-appointed in-
spector of snow storms and rain storms,
and did my duty faithfully; surveyor, if not
of highways, then of forest paths.
— Henry David Thoreau

Background My earliest memories are of walks in the forest behind our house. I have a foggy memory of coming upon a deep gully in the center of thick woods, and to be honest, I'm not sure if it really happened or was part of a dream. But I was in the forest often enough that the memories of trees and streams filled my mind even at three or four, and they remain decades later. I learned much about life through watching the seasons cycle and tadpoles turn into frogs.

It's not as easy to go outside as it is to sit indoors. For one thing, to go outside means to live at nature's temperature rather than the artificial climate we've created for ourselves. But we miss so much of life remaining indoors. A friend of mine lived in the woods in northern Maine for a year. It is one of the coldest regions in the United States, and she went for a walk outdoors every day year-round. If she can do that, surely the rest of us can get outdoors.

Action Take walks in your neighborhood, or if you have access to a park, that's better yet.

Go outside in the morning and watch the sun rise, or watch it set in the evening. The next time there's a full moon, go out and walk in the silvery light. Take someone you love—it's very romantic!

Make hiking or camping a family outing. Teach your children about the local trees and wild-flowers. Take up fishing.

Find *some* excuse to be outside. You'll find it will slow you down and help you live at a better pace of life.

42 ■ Watch for Beauty

You can experience the whole world of beauty in a single flower.
—Henri Nouwen

Background As I entered the busy years of college and career, I lost my early fascination with nature. I was thirty years old before I rediscovered my sense of wonder. Until that time, I didn't know a pansy from a petunia, or a daffodil from an azalea. I was always too busy, too consumed with my big plans and my many worries to take time for such trivial things.

When we bought our first home, the yard was full of flowers. Every day I came home to some new flowers in vases around the house. I began asking my wife their names, and I enjoyed the fragrance of jasmine, narcissus, and gardenias. I began to notice the flowers in the yard, too, and I even took responsibility to fertilize them regularly and watch for pests.

I'm still learning to enjoy flowers, and I'm sorry it took me so long to appreciate them. But this isn't the only example of my insensitivity to beauty. I can still drive home, absorbed with thoughts about my work, and not notice the orange sky at sunset or the golden light on the mountains. I'm happy to say, however, that I do notice my surroundings more often these days.

I can train myself to watch for beauty. And when

I find it, it lifts my heart from its anxious musings and reminds me that there are eternal things in life far more important than my worries or frustrations.

Action   Today, look for every example of beauty you can find. Look for it in the scenery around you. Look for it in artwork. Look for it in the faces of the people you pass on the street. Your life will be richer for it.

When you find beauty, thank God for it, and let it lift your spirits for a moment.

Love and Be Loved

Relationships are eternal. Why then is it so easy to shortchange the ones we love and so easy to overcommit our time to lesser priorities?

43 ▪ Put Your Family First

Background There's a drama being acted out in millions of homes in America. A man works from early morning until late at night six days a week. He sees his children for an hour or two a day, and when he does, he's tired and cranky. As the years pass, his wife's resentment grows; she's raising the children alone. The children view their father like a distant king; he's in command, but if they stay out of his way, they won't bother him, and he won't bother them.

In another version, Mom diligently pursues her own career and leaves the awesome responsibility of raising her children to overworked teachers. Or she spends hours each day on community work, helping others at the expense of those who need her most.

This drama is a tragedy in the classic sense; the players are moved by forces they don't understand. And the children don't know families can be any other way.

One day, the teenagers rebel. There is no firm foundation within the home to weather the storm, and the family begins to disintegrate.

I know several families that have gone through great heartache from precisely this problem. They are not bad people—they sincerely believed they were good parents. Only after a teenage son began to use drugs or a teenage daughter got pregnant did they understand something was wrong.

It's a problem of priorities. Our society places too little value on raising children. "What do you do?" is a question many stay-at-home parents dread. In reality, nothing is more important than the relationship with the ones closest to us.

The belief that it's quality of time—not quantity —is wrong. Your family needs both.

Action Examine your priorities in relationship to your family. Even if you don't have children, do you spend adequate time with your spouse? Watching TV together doesn't count! Do you spend time interacting, having fun together, discussing significant issues?

If you have children, do you invest some of your time in things that are important to them—attending ball games or teaching them to ride a bicycle? Do you *know* what's important to them? Make it a project to learn what they are struggling with, what makes them happiest, and what their hopes are for the future.

As your life becomes simpler, invest more of your time with the people you love. It will pay life-long dividends.

44 ■ Become an Encourager

I expect to pass through this world but once. Any good therefore that I can do, or any kindness that I can show to any fellow creature, let me do it now. Let me not defer or neglect it, for I shall not pass this way again.

—Anonymous

Background   I started a new job once, and like any new employee, I was looking for cues about whether I was doing a good job. Was I catching on as fast as the average new employee? Was I making any obvious blunders?

For months I received almost no feedback, except from one person. This one person told me every time we worked together that I was doing a good that we worked well together. It was no act either; he was sincere. He didn't hesitate to offer criticism either. The criticism was always helpful, and in the context of his encouragement, it was most welcome.

I noticed that this colleague was very popular within the company. Why then is it so hard to emulate his style?

I've tried to learn a lesson from this experience. It takes conscious effort to be an encourager. I'm too distracted and self-absorbed most of the time to notice other people.

Investing in people will greatly improve the quality of your life. My encouraging colleague has as much joy in his life as anyone I know. Being an encourager doesn't take a lot of time; it takes the will to get your eyes off yourself and onto others.

Action What goes around comes around, as the saying goes. It's certainly true with encouragement. If you want to be encouraged, try encouraging others.

It's easy to encourage someone. Just look for something good to say. Everyone has commendable qualities.

Tell your friends something you appreciate about them. Tricia made a list of her friends and wrote down the qualities she most appreciated about each of them. She liked them even more after she did it! She's taking the time to encourage each of them about their good qualities.

We get more satisfaction from being praised for character than for individual incidents. If someone told me she appreciated that I told the truth, that would encourage me, but if she told me she appreciated that I was such an honest person, that would feel even better. Look for praiseworthy character traits in people, and encourage them.

Be especially sensitive to people who are having a bad day. You may be inclined to be rude to people who are rude to you. That is especially true in the marketplace; they don't seem fully human in the role as grocery clerk, flight attendant, or gas station attendant. But say something nice to them, and watch them look at you in disbelief. If you see someone be rude to them, take the opportunity to counteract it.

Become an encourager, and watch it come back around to you.

45 ■ Invest in Edifying Relationships

*A man of many friends comes to ruin,
But there is a friend who sticks closer
than a brother.*

—Proverbs 18:24 NASB

Background The word for "ruin" in the proverb above originally meant "broken into pieces." The proverb is saying, "Don't have too many friends. You'll be broken up into so many pieces that you won't have any friends."

Women get this idea better than men. In surveys, men commonly rate the desire for companionship as the greatest need in their lives. Yet most men by the age of forty have not one person they consider a close friend.

Early in adult life, we begin making attachments that will ultimately become lifelong friends. One of the biggest dangers in the twenties and thirties is that we will invest in too many people. We will be scattered among so many friends that none of the relationships will ever develop into the "friend who sticks closer than a brother."

Ten years ago, Tricia and I developed a close friendship with another couple. We enjoyed Jerome and Dorothy so much that we spent nearly every evening together. We followed that pattern for months, and we often felt guilty about all the friends we were neglecting. Some of our other friends complained; some just stopped calling. I wasn't sure whether we were doing something wrong, but I knew that the kind of friendship we were developing was rare, and I didn't want to let it slip away.

Ten years have passed, and although we aren't together every night—we no longer even live in the same city, in fact—we are certainly best friends for life. In the perspective of ten years, those evenings we spent together were an investment that paid off handsomely.

I now see that there is a principle here. We are finite beings. We can love everyone from a distance, but we can't develop close relationships with more than a few people. These special relationships require time, and we have only so much of it. We must focus our lives on the few people who can be our closest friends.

Even Jesus invested Himself in only twelve disciples. Of those, three were with Him in the most important moments. And there was one special disciple, John, called "the disciple whom Jesus loved."

Action Do you have any close friends, any friends who are as close as brothers? If so, invest in them as a very high priority, second only to the time you spend with your family.

If you don't have such friends, do you know people who are likely candidates? Invest in them! Find time to be with them. Look for ways to encourage them. Look for common interests, and seek to understand what makes them who they are—their hopes, their plans, their struggles.

Let marginal friends slide if need be. Be content to have two levels of friendship: close friends who deserve substantial personal investment and acquaintances who receive minimal effort. Don't let guilt drive you to be a person of many friends, broken into pieces by lack of focus.

46 ■ Love the Unlovable

The biggest disease today is not leprosy or tuberculosis, but rather the feeling of being unwanted, uncared for and deserted by everybody.

—Mother Teresa

Background As the last chapter discussed, we need focus in our relationships if we hope to have close friends. If we share our time with too many people, people will become draining to us. We will find we have little to give to anyone. And we'll go through life without close friends.

However, after building the foundation of close friendships, we don't want to build a fortress around our lives. We need to reach out and give from our abundance to those around us. Life will never be satisfying until we give to others. We need to give to people who are unlovable, those who most need our love and concern.

Tricia and I spent several months in Ethiopia at the height of the famine there in the mid-1980s. That still stands out as one of the highlights of our lives. We worked long hours struggling to get food to the starving masses. Our love for the people overcame all of the horrible conditions and the fear of disease.

The Ministry of Money, in Washington, D.C., organizes several trips a year for what it calls a reverse mission. People travel with them to the

Third World and assist in some program to help the poor. People on the mission consistently report that they receive more from the poor than they give.

Recently, I gave half a sandwich to a homeless person, who said with gratitude, "God bless you!" I was overwhelmed. He had invoked the blessing of the Creator upon me. I had come away with far more than I had given!

Action   Look for people you can touch in some way.

Be one of the first to meet the new neighbor.

Look for the unlovable ones. Befriend the child in the neighborhood the other children don't seem to like. Seek out the person in church others ignore, the one who doesn't dress like the other members.

Look for ways to help the needy. Give them something, or volunteer at a local food bank.

Stop and talk to the homeless person on the street. Many homeless people have said that the worst thing about their condition is the invisibility. People pass them all day and look right through them.

47 ■ Invite a Friend to Join You on the Pilgrimage

A true friend is one soul in two bodies.
—Aristotle

Background The simple life doesn't come easily. The world presses in on you with all its demands and complexity. Your obligations weigh on you. Some steps toward simplicity take courage. You risk being misunderstood for not going along with the crowd. For example, try telling people you don't have a TV, and watch the reaction!

A friend can help. You can struggle together, test ideas with each other, and hold each other accountable.

Action Talk to a friend about simplifying life. If the person seems interested, share this book. Make a commitment to work on these issues together.

Set a regular time to communicate. A friend and I write to each other regularly. When we lived in the same town, we had lunch together once a week.

Push your talk past the clichés, and learn to devote your time to the significant issues in your lives. And be sure to look for ways to encourage each other whenever you are together.

Easy Does It

We were meant to rise above the mundane and
touch the sublime. Don't miss the good things in
life: love, truth, beauty, art.

48 ■■ Stop Seeking Perfection

To live is to feel oneself lost. He who accepts it has already begun to find himself, to be on firm ground.

—Søren Kierkegaard

Background   We were not put on this earth to attain some standard of perfection. The Christian message is one of hope: I'm not okay, you're not okay, but that's okay. Jesus came to redeem us from our imperfection by living the perfect life in our place.

God wants us to seek His character and His presence, not some ideal of perfection. We do not hold our own children to some ideal standard that they must live up to. Rather, we want them to become fully themselves and to learn our values and character. So it is with God. Many have wasted their years striving to live up to imaginary demands of a cosmic dictator. But the Bible says God is love.

If we can release ourselves from believing God demands our perfection, can't we release ourselves from our own demands? Can we give ourselves permission to make mistakes and seek to learn from them? Can we take time to rest, content to let go of some things we had hoped to accomplish?

Action   Seek the will of God, not some imagined perfect plan for your life. I don't believe God's will is a straight line. I think of it as a wide playing field. There are boundaries, but there's a lot of room to express your individuality and make your own choices.

Stop striving for your own standards of perfection. Allow yourself a few bad days here and there. A good friend of mine says, "If I have two hundred good days a year, I'll accomplish great things in my life." It's liberating to allow yourself to read a book and lounge around on a day when you just can't seem to get going. For us Type A personalities, this isn't easy.

Some of us have the freedom to vary our routine even at work. Being an intense worker, my favorite days used to be those where I closed my office door and filled my "out" basket. I finally learned to lighten up and to take walks among the people who work for me. Without exception, that always proves more valuable than anything I could accomplish in my office.

49 ⊞ Go with the Flow

Background   Tricia and I went through some difficult trials for several years related to infertility. We fought against the problem, and were often frustrated and angry.

At the same time, we've had many blessings in our lives. My recent career change went so smoothly as to be almost uncanny. Surveying the last few years, Tricia said, "There are some things in life that just aren't meant to be. No matter how hard you try to make something happen, you are just beating your head against a door. Other things have the ring of inevitability about them. You take a small step, you start to slide, and before you have put out any effort, you've arrived where you wanted to go."

We talked about this idea for weeks. We decided it's one of the keys to enjoying life. The biggest challenge is to have the wisdom to know the difference.

I think this is a life-changing revelation for us. We're trying to be more accepting of what God sends our way. We're trying not to fight so hard to change our circumstances. We want to apply more wisdom, to learn to sense when we've encountered something we can't change. Last year, with very little effort on our part, we adopted twins. It was clearly something that was meant to be.

Action   What things in your life have you fought to change with little or no success? Are they just not meant to be? The apostle Paul spoke about his thorn in the flesh. We aren't sure what it was, but we know he asked God repeatedly to take it away. When it didn't go away, he learned to accept that God was sufficient for him anyway.

Accept that some things in life will never happen —no matter what you do. You can strive for them all your life to no avail, or you can embrace the reality.

Other things in life are just meant to be, and a little effort will bring them to pass. Rejoice in these things.

50 ■ Keep Simplicity Simple

Simplicity may be difficult, but the alternative is immensely more difficult.
—Richard Foster

Background   I said early in this book that simplicity is not easy. Sometimes we're wrestling with the deepest questions in life: Who am I? Why am I here? Sometimes we're going against the grain of our whole society. Occasionally, the family will have differing opinions on how we should handle something.

It's worth the struggle; the rewards are huge. And the struggle doesn't have to make us frantic. We can take it one step at a time. We don't need to do it all today. Simplifying our lives is like peeling an onion—one layer at a time.

All fifty-two suggestions in this book are only that: suggestions. They have worked for Tricia and me. Some will work for you; some won't. All of them cannot possibly be applied in a single week. It's probably wise to work on only one or two at a time.

Action   Don't let your efforts at simplification complicate your life. Take it easy. Work at a reasonable pace.

Get help from family and friends. Don't go it alone.

Simplicity should be a source of joy. The first time you skip your favorite TV shows or drive to the recycling bin, you may not have a hilarious experience. But don't give up. You'll know deep inside if you're on the right track. You'll feel life is fuller.

And if something doesn't work for you, forget it and try something else. Don't get bogged down in your efforts to simplify.

51 ■ Follow Your Bliss

*Let what you do arise out of who you are
. . . whatever I do the rest of my life, it
will not be in order to have an identity. It
will be the result of allowing my God-
given self to emerge.*

—Stan Mooneyham

Background The great philosopher Joseph Campbell summed up his advice to people in this simple phrase: follow your bliss. In it he found the accumulated wisdom of centuries of mythology, fables, and stories.

To follow your bliss means to trust your instincts about what is right for you. That doesn't mean you should ignore morals and conventions, but within the basic framework established by God and society, find the unique path meant for you.

As I said earlier, I believe that if we pray for God's help and seek His character in our lives, we have a wide field to play on. I don't view God's plan for each of us as a razor's edge. One slip and we've left the straight line forever? No, it's not like that.

As we become mature, the choices that are right for us become the ones that give us joy. The deepest part of ourselves, the part created in God's image, yearns to come to the surface. It takes years to clear away the clutter and learn to follow our instincts. But it's worth it. We will not be led astray.

Action Learn to follow your instincts as you depend on God.

Cultivate your interests. If a subject appeals to you, learn about it. If you enjoy something such as art, seek it out.

Find those things that bring joy.

You can't begin to discern these instincts until you have a simple life. Those who spend every moment surrounded by noise or stimulated by television and those who ceaselessly strive to accomplish will never discern them. Simplify your life, and then follow your bliss.